Carl Jung

KNOWLEDGE IN A NUTSHELL

Carl Jung

KNOWLEDGE
IN A
NUTSHELL

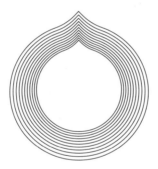

Gary Bobroff

SIRIUS

The author is grateful for the support and assistance
of Liz Jefferson, David Pressault, Elisabeth Pomès,
KD Farris, Stephen Aizenstat, Becca Tarnas,
Alexis Durgee, Marie-Elsa Bragg, Vanessa Scott,
Hanson Shisler, Marigrace Lonergan Gleason
and Sam Gleason, Laura Ferguson and Darcy Riddell.

SIRIUS

This edition published in 2022 by Sirius Publishing, a division of
Arcturus Publishing Limited,
26/27 Bickels Yard, 151–153 Bermondsey Street,
London SE1 3HA

ISBN: 978-1-78950-575-7
AD006861UK

Printed in China

Contents

Introduction

Carl Gustav Jung (1875–1961) was a Swiss psychiatrist and medical doctor. The founder of Analytical Psychology, he is considered one of the intellectual giants of the twentieth century. He was a bestselling author throughout his life and had an enormous influence on Western culture.

His psychology focuses on our inner experience and posits the existence of an unconscious out of which our conscious awareness arises. We experience that unconscious in dreams and other ways, and recognizing it provides a method for better understanding ourselves and others. Jung had been Freud's heir apparent, and while Freud had emphasized the role of sexuality in the unconscious, Jung observed an even more powerful drive in us – the search for meaning. In general, Jungian psychology can be understood as an inquiry into the relationship between consciousness and the unconscious. This method, as practised individually, in analysis and elsewhere, is a dialogue that continues for thousands of people to this day.

This book explores the work of Carl Gustav Jung (referred to as C.G. or Jung), and the living tradition that is Jungian psychology today. It is carried forward by analysts and their analysands, psychotherapists and their patients, and by artists, filmmakers, writers, dancers, business people and others.

The ideas of Swiss psychiatrist Carl Gustav Jung (1875–1961) have been hugely influential.

Jung's approach is about and for the average person; it is a psychology of our everyday lives and every night's dreams. Likewise, this book is intended as a beginner's guidebook. We will explore Jung's primary concepts, focusing on how they're useful, where we can see them in our cultures and why they're relevant today. Where can we see those ideas living around us?

Today, the international Jungian community is an organically growing worldwide phenomenon. Unexpected outgrowths of interest have popped up outside the English-speaking world. You may not be aware that Jung and Freud are very popular across South America; both are taught in college and analysis is commonly undertaken. In Asia, China recently hosted a conference attended by three thousand people, and Korea has a Jung Institute of its own. Perhaps most remarkably, Jung's work bloomed anew in the creative expression of the popular K-pop band BTS. Their album *Map of the Soul: Persona* was based on a book by the Jungian analyst Murray Stein and it explores their own struggles of identity. Their album was such a chart-topper that it drove Stein's book back onto the bestseller list.

The K-pop band BTS released an album based on the work of a Jungian analyst.

That Jung's psychology continues to gain followings in new cultures may be explained by the fact that his primary interest was the universal nature of the psyche.

Jung read ancient Greek and Latin and also spoke German, French and English, among other languages. For a trip to Africa, he taught himself Swahili (and was rewarded with tremendous conversations with tribesmen and shamans about their dreams).

A mandala carved by Jung at Bollingen Tower, a structure he began building after the death of his mother.

He was an open-minded scholar and a person of genuine curiosity. He collected ancient books and medieval alchemical manuscripts. But perhaps what is most remarkable about him is how seriously he took the inner life *as a practice.*

Jung saw inner health as requiring a practice of inner work or dialogue. Early on he began to draw mandalas as a daily form of healing practice. He discovered that using his hands allowed a greater depth of the unconscious to emerge. Crafting images from dreams and visions into paint and wood became for him a form of relationship-building with the unconscious. When he took those voices more seriously, they burst forth, in the period he dubbed Confrontation with the Unconscious. The images of *The Red Book: Liber Novus* depict quite exactly what this experience was like for Jung. Seeing his artwork up close, one is struck by his dedication to the inner world. Art historian Jill Mellick observed that, throughout it all, he gave 'primacy to the process', and he valued 'direct inner experience'.

His was a psychology of inner experience, and it led him first to find out something quite uncomfortable – he had to accept that he was not the master of his own house. He believed our primary awareness to be the central voice in an inner ecosystem of unknown living depth. He likened the unconscious to a stormy sea out of which consciousness emerges. Living there were *complexes*; centres of energy would sometimes split off from conscious awareness and threaten to pull us into them. He saw evidence of these complexes in observations such as the delay times in response to certain words and compulsions, and instances of 'I don't know what came over me'. We sail out into these waters in Chapter 1.

Taking the inner life seriously means listening to more than the ego's voice, and especially including those voices we'd rather not hear. Chief among these is the Shadow – the part of us that we least accept, our inner opposite. Most often this is our bestial self, our least civilized face. *The Strange Case of Dr Jekyll and Mr Hyde* is a classic literary example of this division within us. Our connection to it is experienced as inner conflict, and may remain uncomfortable throughout our lives. It is also, however, a source of energy that can vitalize us. We'll describe how to approach the Shadow in Chapter 2.

How are we best to navigate the dark terrain that is the unconscious? To interpret dreams? To relate to our inner world and the attitude that we should take towards it? How are we best to free ourselves from the terror of our bad dreams? Inner work, dream interpretation and its applications are the subject of Chapter 3.

Jung saw growth into greater expansion and clarity as built into our DNA.[1] At the centre of the psyche's activity was what he called the Self. This is symbolized by centred images of a circle, square or mandala, expressing our inherent drive towards healing and homeostasis. Chapter 4 explores the self-regulating system driving each of us in the search for wholeness.

Jung permeates the culture of the twentieth and twenty-first centuries. So much of the psychological language that we use today comes from him. The way we talk about dreams, archetypes and symbols is because of his work. He coined the terms *complex*, *extravert*, *introvert*, *collective unconscious* and *synchronicity*. Chapter 5 looks at his work on Psychological Types, which gave us the pairs that became the Myers-Briggs Type Indicator™, one of the mostly widely used personality systems in the world.

One of the most profound concepts realized by Jung about the unconscious was the prevalence of patterns that were seemingly not personal. His patients dreamt of strange images that he had seen only in alchemical texts. Living before the age of television and the Internet, Jung could be certain that his patients had never seen them before. Soon he discovered that there were universal strata of archetypal patterns shared by all human cultures. In Chapter 6, we look at archetypes and the collective unconscious – one of the defining discoveries of Jungian psychology.

Jung observed that we have an inner 'other' alive inside of us. We see it in our inner life and in our relationships, and we'll look at it in Chapter 7. Falling in love is sometimes considered a projecting of this figure outwards onto someone else, but in its highest function it can serve to inspire us towards creative construction, to love life and what's best for us, and act as a bridge to the inner Self.

C.G. made the descent into the unconscious and survived, and his work is the catalogue of what he found in that underworld. Discovering archetypes, like natural laws of the psyche, feels a little like brushing the dirt off of an old fossil – something is discovered which was there the whole time and which feels natural and powerful.

Jung wrote steadily throughout his life, and in the 1920s and '30s his books were reviewed in the newspapers of the day. He was discussed by the great writers of the time, including D.H. Lawrence and James Joyce (who brought his daughter to Jung for analysis). Jung was a keen appreciator of the arts, particularly painting and sculpture, and he wrote on art, religion and the wider mysteries and crises of his era.

In 2003, it was revealed for the first time that during the height of World War II Jung was recruited by Allied Intelligence to provide psychological profiles on Axis leaders for them. He was Agent 488 for the Office of Strategic Services (OSS), the American wartime intelligence agency. An analysand of his, Mary Bancroft, was recruited by OSS leader Allen Dulles to be a sometime go-between. He warned that Hitler was a psychopath and should not be underestimated, and his reports were read by General Eisenhower. Dulles later said: 'Nobody will probably ever know how much Prof. Jung contributed to the allied cause during the war.'[2]

Jung's influence on the arts in the post-war world was vast. In Europe, filmmakers such as Bergman and Fellini were inspired by him. In New York, Martha Graham was influenced by the concept of the collective unconscious in her groundbreaking approach to modern dance. In Hollywood, Brando loved him, and in 1955 he appeared on the cover of *TIME* magazine.

The psychological profiles created by Jung during World War II were read by General Eisenhower.

In 1961, he got a letter from Bill Wilson, founder of Alcoholics Anonymous, and in response he made a direct connection between alcoholic compulsion and the thirst for spiritual enlightenment.

Throughout the 1960s Jung was everywhere, including on the cover of The Beatles' *Sgt. Pepper's Lonely Hearts Club Band*. The Doors were reading him too, and The Rolling Stones infamously explored his concept of the Shadow in 'Sympathy For The Devil'. His books were widely read, and he has outsold Freud two to one since the beginning. He used divination throughout his life, particularly the Chinese *I Ching* three-coin method, and he wrote the foreword for a book on the subject published by Princeton University Press in 1967. This association, along with his interest in extended mind phenomena, synchronicity, astrology and other esoteric topics, made him a huge part of the counterculture movements in the 1960s and the later New Age movement.

In the 1970s, James Hillman developed his own branch of the family tree with Archetypal Psychology, and Joseph Campbell's Jung-influenced mythology books became popular. Campbell and Jung's writing on the Hero archetype came directly into play in George Lucas's 1977 blockbuster, the iconic *Star Wars*. And in 1983, The Police had a Number One hit album with *Synchronicity*.

About this time, two of the most celebrated women writers of the Jungian family emerged. Marion Woodman wrote about the price that Western culture pays for its loss of connection to the archetypal feminine in *Addiction To Perfection: The Still Unravished Bride* (1982) and *The Owl Was a Baker's Daughter: Obesity, Anorexia Nervosa, and the Repressed Feminine* (1980). In 1989, Clarissa Pinkola Estés debuted her now classic *Women Who Run With the Wolves: Myths and Stories about the Wild Woman Archetype* (1989). In the 1990s, Hillman, along with other Jungian-influenced writers Thomas Moore and James Hollis, hit the bestseller list too. They all led readers back to tending their inner world in daily life. These very popular authors and their many millions of readers are a part of the measure of Jung's ultimate impact.

Jung discussed synchronicity and the nature of reality with master physicists Albert Einstein and Wolfgang Pauli, starting as early as 1911. In the phenomenon of synchronicity, he saw that the subject was capable of having an effect on the objective world through their inner state, a view shared with both ancient Taoism and the modern physicists who kept finding the observer's fingerprints in the quantum dust that they observed. Chapter 8 asks what it means when reality allows circumstances to come together in meaningful ways.

In 1944, while recovering from a heart attack, Jung wrote an analysis of the Western God image, called *Answer to Job*. He noted that throughout the Bible the human characters drive the moral development. He understood this as bringing humanity into an active role in the divine drama, providing a cosmic dignity to the struggle of life and offering a meaningful and satisfying answer to why there is evil in the world. These 'Big Questions' are also explored in Chapter 8.

Jung directly influenced the way the twentieth century saw itself. In addition to developing a school of psychology, his insights helped to inspire some of our best-loved films, music and books. Today, this psychodynamic point of view is one of the key tenets of art appreciation and is used daily in marketing, politics, literature and entertainment. At the end of this book, in the first appendix we'll examine Jung's involvement in World War II, and in the second, entitled 'A Field Guide to Jung Today', we'll look at some of the pioneers taking this work forward into the twenty-first century.

Perhaps the reason that Jung's work remains popular is that he offers a meaningful framework for approaching the biggest questions of our time. A *New York Times* review of *The Undiscovered Self* in 1997 described the book as 'a passionate plea for individual integrity'. Jung believed that our inner personal work was the only thing that could save us from the great danger – ourselves. In the face of today's challenges, it remains within the power of every individual to be 'the makeweight that tips the scales'.[3] The ultimate reason that we're still talking about Jung today is because of how seriously he took the inner life. May this book inspire you to realize how important yours is too.

Carl Jung discussed his ideas on synchronicity with leading scientists of the time, such as Albert Einstein.

CHAPTER 1
Jung's Psychology

WHERE DID JUNG COME FROM?

Carl Gustav Jung was born in Kesswil, Switzerland, on 26 July 1875. He was named after his grandfather who had been an illustrious physician (and who may have been the illegitimate son of Goethe).

C.G.'s father was a pastor, as were eight of his uncles. This brought him close to funeral rites and death from an early age. When he was just six months old, his mother developed a nervous disorder and was separated from him for several months. His mother and maternal grandfather (also a respected pastor) were spiritualists who spoke to the spirits of the departed – a practice that was not uncommon among the rural Swiss of his time. When he grew older, C.G. realized that his father's faith did not animate him, nor fill his life with meaning. That absence struck C.G. profoundly, and the split between his mother's mediumistic side and his father's unfulfilled religiosity would define his life.

Two elder children had died before he was born, and C.G. had no siblings until he was nine. Growing up as a solitary child, he spent a great deal of time alone and involved in fantasy. He had several powerful dreams that he would write about later in his life, including one of a fleshy, tree-like pillar. A dreamy young boy, he grew up into a sturdy and fiery red-haired young man.

When he was four years old, his family moved to Basel, a Swiss city known for its tremendous carnival, the largest in Europe. For three days, beginning at 4 am, thousands of masked revellers paraded through town – a ritual that continues to this day.

His father died when he was 20, and he was invited to a séance shortly after, at which his 15-year-old cousin channelled spirits. Around the same time, two paranormal events struck C.G.'s family home: the splitting of a table down the middle for no apparent reason, and the shattering of a knife that was inside a drawer (a knife he kept for the rest of his life). C.G. felt that these events were somehow related to the death of his father.

C.G. won a scholarship and studied at Basel University, where he had a passion for science, philosophy and archaeology. He read Kant, Nietzsche and Swedenborg, and was a member of the Zofingia Club, an intellectual debating group, from 1896 to 1899.

In 1900, he moved to Zurich and began his medical studies. In 1903, he married Emma Rauschenbach (1882–1955), the daughter of one of the wealthiest families in Switzerland. Together they would have four daughters and one son. Their home in Küsnacht was the centre of both his family life and psychological practice, and today his descendants have made it available for private tours.

C.G. was a warm and vital person. He enjoyed physical pursuits, drinking wine and smoking cigars and a pipe. He was magnetic, witty and charming. He liked playing games, and his personality type was more the brother than the patriarchal father figure. A later biographer would write: 'Everyone who came into

Carl Jung and his wife Emma Rauschenbach. The pair were married on 14 February 1903.

A 19th-century illustration of the Basel Carnival. The carnival was one of the largest in Europe.

personal contact with Jung has commented on his joviality, the twinkle in his eyes, his hearty, infectious laugh and his wonderful sense of humour. He was a good listener and . . . never appeared to be hurried or preoccupied. In conversation he was tolerant of different points of view, flexible in his approach to questions, and simple in speech . . . People felt comfortable in his presence.'[4]

C.G.'s laugh was so infectious that his secretary Aniela Jaffé told the story of a hiker who, travelling the road above Eranos, a research centre in Switzerland, heard laughter from high above in the mountains and had to come and investigate who this man was.[5]

In 1910, following the death of her father and her subsequent depression, Toni Anna Wolff (1883–1953) began working with Jung as an analysand. C.G. helped her with her depression and she became one of his greatest helpers and closest confidantes. She was gifted intellectually and psychologically, and when he descended into his period of 'Confrontation with the Unconscious', just before and during World War I, she was able to assist him to get through it. Wolff was his 'psychic lifeguard' during his time of greatest difficulty, and she became a great psychoanalyst herself – better, some said, than Jung.

In 1922, following the death of his mother, C.G. bought land at Bollingen on Lake Zurich. The following year, he began construction there of a stone tower that was his refuge from the business of family life and society. At his tower, he chopped his own firewood, cooked his own meals and had time for introspection and to get in touch with his inner voice. This refuge was a place of great importance to Jung. On and off throughout his life he lectured and taught at Swiss universities. His writing would make him one of the best-known thinkers of the twentieth century and he would be given honorary degrees by many prestigious American and European universities. He kept a vast correspondence with friends and prominent figures around the world. He died at the age of 86 at his home in Küsnacht, on 6 June 1961.

A photograph of the entrance to Bollingen Tower. Jung continued to extend the building throughout his life.

THE PSYCHOLOGY OF JUNG

The psychology of Carl Gustav Jung unfolds a vast interior world living inside of us. To begin to describe that territory is daunting. Imagine a hologram of our Milky Way galaxy: swirling around, with heights and depths of moving celestial bodies. How to begin to talk about it? How to place it all in a linear fashion (a, b, c, etc)? I ask the reader's forgiveness as we begin – while it's exciting to get to the conceptual parts of Jung's work, we must begin simply and answer some basic questions first. We will take personal psychology as our starting point in this chapter, as it is the closest to our own experience.

THE WORD ASSOCIATION EXPERIMENT

In 1900, after completing his medical studies, Jung began work at the Burghölzli psychiatric hospital in Zurich. A resident in psychiatry, Jung was supervised by Dr Eugen Bleuler, a leading figure in European psychiatry. It was here that Jung made his first original contribution to psychology – the Word Association Experiment.

In the search for an empirical way to evaluate the conditions underlying patient's illnesses, Jung developed an experiment in which patients were read a series of words and asked to free associate – respond with the first thing that came to their mind. At first, he had no success. Following Bleuler's lead, Jung had expected associations for certain words to correlate with particular diseases, but they did not. Only after accepting the experiment's initial failure did a revealing quality appear to Jung within the test results.

Jung noticed that certain words caused patients to delay in their response; it would take longer than the typical 1 to 3 seconds for them to respond. This break in attention was telling; it hinted at something present beneath the surface. Exploring, he found that the delay often occurred alongside changes in facial expression, spontaneous movements, emotional response and other reactions that defied the experiment's instructions. In the laboratory setting, Jung was able to use instruments to observe the presence of physical symptoms connected to this disruption, which provided evidence of emotional response. 'He used measures of changes in the pulse rate, fluctuations in breathing, and changes in the electrical conductivity of the skin produced by emotional sweating, in conjunction with the word-association test.'[6]

In one example, the word 'horse' brought a delay of over a minute. It came out that the participant had been in a runaway horse accident, which they had completely forgotten. This was an example of a difficult experience that had been pushed out of awareness. It was too difficult to bear and was repressed. 'Repression is an unnoticed, that is an unconscious, response to a

Eugen Bleuler was the director of the Burghölzli clinic, and he was a great influence on Jung.

conscious situation. Yet the conflict has not vanished; it remains active below the surface of consciousness and may, to our surprise and distress, produce symptoms.'[7]

Carl Jung standing outside the Burghölzli clinic, a psychiatric hospital in Zurich, where he worked from 1900 to 1909.

This discovery pointed Jung towards something that was operating beneath the surface of awareness. He would soon coin the term *complex* (initially, the *feeling-toned complex*) to describe this force in the psyche. The delay that occurred came about because a complex had been struck.

To this day, a delay in response is one of the primary tools used by intelligence officers and border guards in assessing whether someone is lying to them. The papers that Jung published on the Word Association Experiment would bring him his first recognition in America.

THE COMPLEX

Carl Jung's Association Experiment revealed that there were forces within us which could cause us to respond unusually or even fail to respond at all in the face of certain stimuli. Particular words were capable of interrupting our flow of attention or of blocking us from behaving in the way that we wanted. Jung noticed that these blockages were nearly always also connected to emotion.

The term *complex* was an original contribution to modern psychology. A complex

THE ASSOCIATION METHOD   221

An Example of Normal Reaction Type—Cont.

Stimulus word	Reaction Time Unit 0.2 second	Reaction	Reproduction
stem	6	flower	
to dance	9	I	like
lake	8	Zurich	
sick	8	sister	
pride	6	people	
to cook	7	woman	
ink	5	black	
angry	10	children	people
needle	9	to prick	
to swim	10	healthy	
voyage	9	England	
blue	10	pretty	like
lamp	6	light	
to sin	8	much	people
bread	10	good	like, necessary
rich	9	nice	
tree	6	green	
to prick	9	need	

An Example of an Hysterical Reaction Type

Stimulus word	Reaction Time Unit 0.2 second	Reaction	Reproduction
needle	7	to sew	
to swim * †	9	water	ship
voyage	35	to ride, motion, voyager	
blue	10	color	
lamp	7	to burn	
to sin	22	this idea is totally strange to me, I do not recognize it	
bread	10	to eat	
rich †	50	money, I don't know	possession
brown	6	nature	green
to prick	9	needle	
pity	12	feeling	
yellow	9	color	
mountain	8	high	
to die	8	to perish	
salt	15	salty (laughs) I don't know	NaCl
new	15	old	as an opposite
custom	10	good	barbaric
to pray	12	Deity	
money	10	wealth	
foolish	12	narrow minded, restricted	?
pamphlet	10	paper	

* Denotes misunderstanding.   † Denotes repetition of the stimulus words.

Tables from 'The Association Method' by Carl Jung, published in The American Journal of Psychology, *1910.*

29

is a locus of psychic energy that operates autonomously beneath our awareness. Acting like a magnet, a complex pulls our attention in directions it might otherwise not want to go. The intensity of our emotional response is a measure of the strength of the complex and the degree of its power within us. Jung saw the nucleus of a complex as being intense feeling and, like a psychological wound, you feel 'its effects, even though you don't know the meaning and the cause of the suffering'.[8]

One way in which we can observe a complex in action is through a disturbance in our behaviour. Today, we speak of a Freudian slip as a verbal faux pas that reveals an inner truth often hidden even from the speaker themselves. This is an example of a complex in action, and in 1907 Freud himself began using this term, replacing the term *circles of thought* in later editions of his book *The Psychopathology of Everyday Life* (originally published in 1901).

This compulsive nature of the complex is something that nearly all of us have experienced. Moments of 'I don't know what came over me' are nearly universal, but happen most often when a feeling value is at stake (even if that value is unconscious to us in the moment). In Jungian psychology, feeling is recognized as a measure of the true value of how important something is to us – whether we would like it to be or not. Jung wrote that the complex 'behaves like an animated foreign body', and cannot be argued out of existence or washed away by an effort of will (at least, not for very long).

Complexes are sometimes witnessed in exaggerated reactions or by the absence of a response where one should be expected. A complex may come through in a particularly negative attitude towards something, which hides a rejected inner desire. Sometimes we overcompensate, trying too hard to show that we're not affected by something – and our behaviour reveals otherwise. A classic line from Shakespeare's *Hamlet* – 'The lady doth protest too much, methinks' – refers to just this kind of strong denial that speaks to a hidden truth. It's not uncommon for others to notice a complex acting through us before we recognize it in ourselves.

An illustration of a scene from Shakespeare's Hamlet. *The famous line 'The lady doth protest too much, methinks' tells of the typical overcompensation that results from denial.*

The term *complex* was an original contribution to modern psychology by C.G. Jung. Today, we hear it used in terms such as an *inferiority complex*, referring to someone who unknowingly sees themselves as worse than others, or a *power complex*, referring to someone who seeks control over others. In fact, such complexes are often part of our character and can even be a constitutional element of our personality. A complex may originate in personal pain that has been repressed over the course of a lifetime and it may build up in pressure. It is often this pressure that leads an individual to therapy. 'Reality sees to it that the peaceful cycle of egocentric ideas is constantly interrupted by ideas with a strong feeling-tone, that is, by affects.'[9] Despite our rational self-conception, the complex points us to a deeper force operating within us: the existence of the unconscious.

THE UNCONSCIOUS

The idea of the unconscious had been discussed for centuries, but it was Freud and Jung who brought it into common use in the twentieth century.

After realizing what he had found with the Word Association Experiment, Jung rushed to read Freud's *The Interpretation of Dreams*. There, he found a parallel to his own work. Freud saw repressed contents active in dreams – powerful forces at work within us beneath our awareness – and thus began a period where each psychologist's efforts reinforced the other.

Jung began to follow Freud's work avidly and started a study group among his colleagues. After some time, a correspondence began between them, and at one point Freud was in such a rush to read Jung's work on the Word Association Experiment that he went out and bought a copy rather than wait for the one sent to him by Jung in the mail! In 1907, they finally met face to face at Freud's home, and famously spoke uninterrupted for 13 hours. Jung soon became integrated into the psychoanalytic movement in Vienna, and eventually became Freud's heir apparent.

Freud saw dreams as expressing hidden wishes that are unacceptable, either to us or to society. For him, dream images were transformations of literal instincts into a disguised form. For Jung and Freud, the unconscious was an objective reality as independent from us as the outer world. The power of the unconscious was clearly apparent to both men. They were dealing with patients who had been overtaken by forces within themselves. They saw neuroses (impaired functioning, helplessness, anxiety, depression, obsession) as psychic energy that had become tied up in the unconscious. There was a conflict at work beneath the surface of awareness, one that could not be willed away, a disconnection between inner reality and outer attitude.

Witnessing these effects, Jung observed, 'one does not have a complex, a complex has him'.[10] The voices heard by a psychotic patient are a complex made audible. A powerful dream of someone might be seen as a personification of a complex. A complex has its own energy, and is a split-off piece of consciousness. It may even be considered to be a partial personality within us, and it is this kind of fragmentation that lies behind nervous breakdowns.

Both Jung and Freud saw dreams and symptoms as expressing an attempt at healing from within the psyche. Something that could not be integrated was split off and expressed itself in symbolic form. Psychological illnesses could be understood and cured through recognizing and relating to these voices inside of us. Psychoanalysis (as Freud's work is called) or Analytical Psychology (as Jung's would later be called) promoted the healthy interrelating of consciousness and the unconscious. Jung and Freud turned our attention towards the forgotten inner life inside us, and changed the way that we viewed ourselves. The two men gave us a new language for discussing the forces operating beneath the activity of the conscious mind.

THE SYMBOLIC NATURE OF THE PSYCHE

Freud and Jung both observed that the unconscious spoke in the language of symbol, image, analogy and metaphor.

Sigmund Freud was a great influence on Jung, who at first became an enthusiastic member of the emerging psychoanalytic movement.

For Freud, symbolic images in dreams represented discernible contents from the unconscious. It is a kind of cliché today to equate all cylindrical images with the male phallus, but that example reflects the kind of direct mechanism between image and object which Freud had in mind. For him, dream images only thinly disguised a definable hidden object. He saw the unconscious as a kind of dark mirror reflecting repressed contents back to us; all we needed to do was to decode them properly, and healing could be found. Jung came to believe that this view risked not only misunderstanding the meaning of those symbols but also avoiding seeing something very important about the nature of our inner life.

Jung saw Freud's approach as reducing a symbol to a sign – for example, the cigar as penis. The image referred directly to a lost object and its appearance was caused by this loss; dream contents were only a representation of a past desire gone underground, and never more than a 'substitute for the real thing.'[11] While Jung followed Freud in viewing the images produced by the unconsciousness as compensatory for the repressed experiences of our daytime lives, he also saw them as something more. The activity of the psyche revealed something far deeper, more dynamic and more purposive living inside us.

In addition to Freud's retrospective view of the image's purpose, Jung also saw a prospective, forward-looking function. The images of the unconscious were capable of anticipating future achievements of consciousness and outlining solutions to conflicts.[12] 'The symbol is not a sign that everybody knows. Such is not its significance; on the contrary it attempts to elucidate, by means of analogy, something that still belongs entirely to the domain of the unknown or something that is yet to be.'[13] Such images point to a living process of real psychological growth within us, a development which the conscious mind is not yet capable of appreciating. Symbols straddle the conscious mind and the unconscious, and both our conflict and its solution; they point towards future growth that transcends our current state of being.

This is one of the ways that Jung saw the images produced by the psyche as symbols in the truest sense of the word – they point to a range of possibilities beyond a singular literal interpretation. For example, Freud's Oedipal theory that explained dreams of incest as a repressed desire for the possession of our own mothers could be understood instead as the desire for deeper contact with mothering qualities inside ourselves. Jung believed that such dreams did not point to a desire for literal incest, but rather represented an interior process of integration and even a spiritual rebirth springing from contact with the ground of the unconscious inside us. (For Jung, the mother was associated with the basis of the unconscious itself.) That conclusion is possible only by moving beyond seeing images as only signs. Recognizing a symbol's coherence requires an intuitive appreciation of the unity in these various meanings. That appreciation requires a type of thinking beyond literal understanding.

The most powerful symbols draw profound reactions from us. The symbolic images in great art attract and fascinate us; they stir our souls and move us beyond what can be easily expressed: 'their pregnant language cries out to us that they mean more than they say.'[14]

The unconscious produces symbols as part of a natural process within us. These images emerge out of the context of our lived experience. The image of the horse has a very different meaning for someone who rides everyday than it does for the dreamer mentioned earlier, whose only experience is having fallen off and been hurt. Thus, systems that equate images with a particular literal meaning for everyone are unlikely to generate profound healing within us. Jung saw the meaning-making process as one that not only requires attendance to the real context of our particular lives and history, but also involves profound inner listening. It asks us to use our rational capacities, but also our feeling and imaginal ones.

Symbolic images redirect our psychic energy, bringing together conscious and unconscious material and producing the lessening of conflict. In this way, they activate a transcendent function within the psyche. We experience this as the discovery of personal meaning and healing. This transformation is not the result of formulaic operations, but rather is a dynamic process that requires our authentic and vulnerable participation. The process challenges the whole of who we are and requires deep moral effort. That the unconscious would produce moving, powerful compensatory symbols inside us at all points to a fact that our culture may still not have fully grasped – that there is a force working within us which is always driving us towards healing growth and greater consciousness.

These differences in approach to symbols would become a contributing factor in Jung's split from Freud, and mirrored their differing views of the psyche. For Freud, consciousness was primary and the unconscious was a kind of basement of lost contents. Jung, instead, saw the unconscious as the matrix out of which consciousness emerged – the tip of an iceberg, a cork bobbing on top of the ocean of the unconscious.

What Jung called the *psyche* was both consciousness and the unconscious. He would come to see this larger whole as compensatory, self-regulating and purposive. He saw an active drive towards uniting consciousness and the unconscious alive within us – we are driven to encompass more of that whole. He would call that drive *individuation* and its by-product *wholeness*. Despite our suffering, the psyche is always ultimately seeking both a healthy homeostatic balance and our ever-unfolding growth and unique development.

WELTANSCHAUUNG – ONE'S VIEW OF LIFE

Jung believed that our psychological health is directly related to our attitude towards life. Our *Weltanschauung*, or philosophy of life, produces our wellness or difficulties, and it is rooted in both consciousness and the unconscious. Our way of understanding the world or attitude towards life is a quality of both outer adaptation and inner predisposition. Our feeling towards something is more

A scene from Oedipus at Colonus, *a play by Sophocles. The story of Oedipus was at the heart of one of Freud's most famous theories, the so-called Oedipus complex.*

important than what that something is. Our *raison d'être* affects us profoundly. 'I have frequently seen people become neurotic when they content themselves with inadequate or wrong answers to the questions of life.'[15] Jung's approach to psychological work was focused on developing that inner attitude. This means that it is necessary for us to become aware of what our own particular *Weltanschauung* is.

In this way, Jungian psychology is not a technique nor a methodology. There is no single map of growth to which we are all made to adhere. Quite the opposite, in fact. It is our particular development that must be furthered, not the fulfilment of any kind of exterior model or outer ideal of personality. This is different from many other schools of psychology, both then and now. Jung felt that far too often our philosophies of life are one-dimensional and they leave us unbalanced. 'If making money is an end in itself, both science and art can quietly shut up shop. No one can deny that our modern consciousness, in pursuing these mutually exclusive ends, has become hopelessly fragmented. . . . trained to develop only one quality they become tools themselves.'[16] Many modern psychologies seek to reinforce a particular kind of development, while Jung's approach is predicated upon a curious openness to the individual's own unique unfolding. For Jung, there is no ideal form of normality, no single right way to be. In this way, his view of human nature challenged conventional notions of right personhood (as did Freud's). In focusing on our relationship to our woundedness, inner life and capacity for growth, Jung also highlighted our uniqueness.

The discovery of the unconscious required a new view of ourselves. We were no longer the master of our own house. This radical new understanding is arguably still not fully grasped by our culture today. 'We are all much more than "I" of whom we are aware.'[17] The unconscious holds the blueprint of who we are and the task of unfolding that pattern requires a relationship to inner forces within us. At the same time that Jung and Freud were doing their early pioneering work, physicists in the same part of

Carl Jung highlighted the importance of our worldview, or Weltanschauung, to our mental wellbeing.

the world were also discovering a connection between inner and outer. In an historic parallel, physicists were finding a relation between the observer and the observed in the quantum universe. Both of these fields would lead us to begin questioning the illusion of pure objectivity and change how we look at our world.

Jung and Freud both observed that much of what ails us today is a product of being split off from our inner life. Healing that inner division requires us to speak the language of symbol, and that necessitates a kind of thinking which is not easy for many of us. This kind of approach is particularly challenging in our culture, which has a bias in favour of the too bright, daylight awareness of the conscious mind, and privileges literal thinking and mechanistic ways of understanding the world.

Key Points

- **Word Association Experiment** – a test devised by Jung which reveals the existence of autonomous complexes within the psyche.

- **The Complex** – a feeling-toned centre of psychic energy that operates autonomously beneath our awareness.

- **The Unconscious** – a layer of psychic functioning below the threshold of consciousness, and the matrix out of which ego self-awareness emerges. Complexes and other centres of energy exist in the unconscious.

- **Symbolic Nature of the Psyche** – the unconscious produces symbolic images that redirect our psychic energy, bring together conscious and unconscious material, and produce the lessening of conflict. In this way, they perform a transcendent function within the psyche.

- *Weltanschauung* – our attitude towards life, which contributes to our psychological health and is rooted in both the conscious and unconscious mind.

CHAPTER 2
The Shadow

'PLEASED TO MEET YOU'

Jung took as his first principle the discovery by Freud that psychological suffering is rooted in the conflict 'between the instinctive nature of people and the demands imposed upon them by the society in which they live.'[18] Symptoms are seen as arising most often out of the friction between human nature and societal code.

Our families and cultures set parameters around which behaviours, thoughts and feelings are allowed. Messages are sent, via both parents and schools, which cordon off parts of who we are. As a natural part of development, there builds up in each of us an inner figure who holds the shame and pain of early life's unpleasant accommodation into the world. That figure expresses itself later in our experience of painful inner states.

Our ideas of shame, guilt and sin live in this emotional terrain within us. This same conflict is the primary concern of religion and literature. It is the place of our highest aspirations and disappointing realities. But, in addition to symptoms, its other by-product is growth in morality. This pointed conflict is lived inside us – and in the world every day.

Where there is a conflict, there are two characters at war, two forces vying, and this rejected figure is the internal adversary,

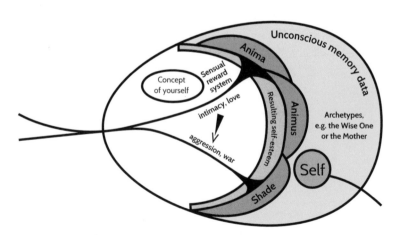

A diagram of Carl Jung's model of the psyche.

The murder of Abel by his brother Cain. Stories of conflict have fascinated us for centuries.

the enemy inside of us. From Cain and Abel to Dr Jekyll and Mr Hyde, stories of hostile brothers hold a strong fascination for us.

If our conscious awareness is the inner hero, this force is the inner villain. If you ask: 'Is this all there is to it?' and insist: 'I'll just defeat him!', you may be underappreciating his nature. He's the worst part of ourselves, our inner betrayer, and applying your willpower may not be enough.

We are very inclined not to look at this part of ourselves – we always begin by pushing it onto others before we see it in ourselves. Yet it is a part of us that we need to make contact with; a part we need to hear out. It is our pain, which we've forgotten about. It is the active presence of the traumas that we carry. But it is also a universal constituent element in the psyche of everyone; it is the countervailing force to ego's self-identity, an inner opposite sunk deep and giving our personality ballast. But part of it is also bigger than our personal experience; it is the entry point for a timeless force. It has a collective expression and even an archetypal reality that must be faced in the course of maturity.

Jung's insight was to discover something that we so often see in fairy tales: in becoming able to name the villain, we are freed somewhat from its power. As in the story of Rumpelstiltskin, it is by exploring the monster's territory and making contact that we gain the insight that transforms the situation. The monster is a puzzle to be solved symbolically, but we must also learn to relate to him; we must learn his name, for it is ours too.

While the monster may be just a figment of our imagination, the power it holds is very real. Reconnecting often brings with it an increased flow of energy.

The early experiences that form us not only affect our views of good and bad, but also unconsciously define our feelings about the nature of the world, our spiritual, religious and philosophical preferences. Where do you put the darkness? It is out of the most rejected parts of ourselves that climb the scariest monsters of our imagination, including our unconscious beliefs about the nature of reality and God.

PERSONA

A word derived from Latin, *persona* originally referred to the masks worn by the actors in ancient classical theatre. In Jungian psychology, this term refers to the inner character that we use to face the world. Drawn from societal expectations, cultural norms and natural attributes, it is both the person we think we ought to be and the person we want others to think we really are. Our persona is our brave face, our false front. It is the ongoing project of building our ideal self.

There are myriad influences on us through our lifetime, from parents, siblings and schools to marketing and media constantly telling us how and who we should be. The persona is our successful adaptation to that pressure.

Our ego (our conscious self, our daytime self-awareness) is closely related to, but not equivalent with, the persona. 'Ego functioning is always, to a certain extent, overlaid with a certain amount of persona.'[19]

A healthy persona allows us to move through the world more easily. It allows us to navigate relationships, community and business life. Growth through many stages of early adult life depend on a solid persona achievement:

A persona is necessary; it clothes the individual in a way that can help the usual observer come to an appropriate idea of what that person is like. I would say that if you are going to present a gift of a diamond ring, you would not package it in a paper bag, and if you were going to give someone a quart of milk, you would probably not choose to give it in a crystal flask. The purpose of the persona is to indicate something of what the person is like, just as the mask suggests the role or emotions of the actor. It has its part in facilitating an adaptation to the requirements of society.[20]

While the persona is an expression of cultural adaptation, it can take a countercultural form. We're exposed to a wide range of cultural norms today, compelling us in different directions and offering us various ways of expressing ourselves. However, some cultures apply even greater emphasis and strictness on this process. Japan, for example, has intricate traditions designed for saving face and avoiding public embarrassment. Much of this is dependent on proper respect being shown to others and correct attendance to their status. All such rituals are made in the service of the persona and status structure.

Does how you appear in society define your place? In the quest for status, status symbols will often do. Your persona is the way you present yourself to the world, but it is also the part of us that may confuse our inner worth with our outer appearance. Jung wrote that the temptation to be what one seems to be is great 'because the persona is usually rewarded in cash'.[21] Cultures have their own particular forms for this. In Los Angeles, for example, the joke is that you're judged by how nice your car is. Designer clothes, big houses and 'keeping up with the Joneses' can be persona expressions. One of the dangers of identifying with the persona can be boastfulness, acting like you're more than you really are.

While the persona is strongly connected to our ego, it is also a complex in its own right. As a complex, it is something that may trap us. We can become too invested in our persona and, in doing so, become unable to see the other parts of who we are. 'The stronger and more rigid the persona, the more we identify with it, the more we must deny the other important aspects of our personality.'[22]

The persona can be a too-dominant inner King or Queen, an inner Ruler that focuses us on facade. If we're psychologically invested in seeing ourselves and having others see us as the Good Guy, we might be touchy about others telling us we're not. We see this maintenance of the persona with gurus or cult leaders, for example, or parents in rigid family systems. There is often a conspiracy to silence anyone who speaks ill of the leader and a concerted effort to keep him or her from being confronted with their shadow. Of course, such social conditions empower the acting out of the dark side.

The persona can be a domineering King or Queen, demanding that we maintain our outside image.

THE SHADOW

One night in the early 1880s, Robert Louis Stevenson dreamt of a good doctor who discovered a potion that made a very different version of himself come to life. The dream became *The Strange Case of Dr Jekyll and Mr Hyde*, a story whose central character with a split self remains easy for audiences to identify with to this day.

Dr Jekyll is a philanthropist, an idealist, too good for the other characters to believe. When he takes the potion and transforms, out emerges Mr Hyde, the uncivilized version of himself. Hyde is unabashed and takes what he wants, knows no limits. He does what is not to be done.

It is appropriate that this captivating story came from a dream, because it is one of our most perfect illustrations of the inner complexes: *persona* and *shadow*. The *persona* is our somewhat embellished view of ourselves, the shiny face that we like the world to see. Its opposite, everything we reject about ourselves, is called the *shadow*.

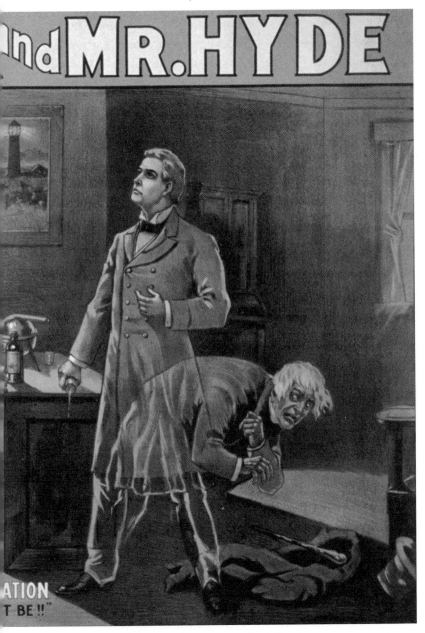

Like Dr Jekyll and Mr Hyde, the persona and shadow represent two opposing parts of our personality.

In Dr Jekyll we have the *persona*: our best notion of who we could be and hope to be, our idealized view of who we are. He treats sick patients for free, avoids being too forward with women, and is a vision of bright moral progressiveness. In Mr Hyde, all the repressed behaviours are acted out, and the opposing values are expressed too – a perfect illustration of the *shadow*.

The development of a civilized persona, the light side of the ego, leaves behind the aggressive, instinctual self within us, but also often our spontaneity, strong emotions and connections to the inner life. The shadow embodies all that is rejected in us, and particularly that which the ego cannot abide – what you have been taught by society and parents to believe is bad.

In the way we speak today, we use the term *shadow* to be nearly synonymous with the unconscious. To say that something is in the shadow is intended to mean that it is unconscious. However, in Jungian use this means a specific complex that each of us has alive within us – an inner rejected other.

The shadow is a same-sex inner figure, who personifies everything about ourselves that we reject. Shadow compensates for the persona and is the opposite of our ego. The ego, shadow and persona can be understood as coming into formation together dynamically throughout our childhood and teenage years. They continue to interrelate similarly throughout our lives.

Our shadow is the pain we've forgotten about. It is a complex within us, a split-off part of our consciousness loaded with emotional weight. Our persona is what we most want to be seen to be; shadow is what we least want to be. When we come into contact with our shadow, our ego's underbelly, it brings into question the bright self-image of the persona.

The shadow is not just the opposite of ego, but 'rather what each conscious personality lacks',[23] and in this way it also affects our view of others. Each of us is gifted in only so many possible ways, and each of us has differing limits and capacities. As with Jekyll and Hyde, the shadow is our inner hostile sibling and represents what we are missing, and in that way it naturally affects

The shadow represents everything we reject about ourselves, and affects how we view the world.

our relationship to our own gender. What we admire or dislike in other men or women often reflects our own hidden face. That rejected part of ourselves is most often first encountered through *projecting* it onto others.

SHADOW PROJECTION

Projection is the psychological mechanism by which our inner contents are invested in outer figures. When we project, we displace an energy or figure inside ourselves onto someone who fits its image in some way. When you meet someone who really triggers you, whether it is love at first sight or an immediate dislike, it is possible that a projection is underway. Sometimes we meet someone who matches the nature or character of our inner complexes and we immediately unconsciously dress them to match our inner image. When this happens, we are *constellated* – brought into dynamic alignment with an inner figure. (But we don't know it; we only know how we feel.)

We project the shadow, for example, onto someone who happily expresses the qualities that are most difficult for us to express. We might find we dislike such a person, although we may not see why at the time. 'Everything that irritates us about others can lead us to an understanding of ourselves.'[24] For example, the bully hates the nerd because their intelligence may be his own area of weakness. This is the dynamic of scapegoating – the innocent is blamed for the crime in order to protect the guilty; one is chosen to be taken in place of ourselves. When we project, we psychologically and emotionally invest something of ourselves in an outer person who then bears that quality for us.

It can be a tremendous relief to project onto others. When we identify with the Hero and see ourselves as the Good One, the fight against the Bad One becomes a righteous act. Remember, for centuries moral rightness could be decided on the field of battle. Such emotional investiture allows us to participate in the combat vicariously and feel good. The Good One's goodness is our goodness, and our goodness becomes theirs – and we no longer remember our less-than-perfect real selves. If the Bad One fits just right, he'll carry the weight of our inner discomfort for a moment and we will feel relieved. 'It is He who does bad things,' we tell ourselves, 'not me.'

Shadow projection is the start of a natural process by which we are invited to discover something inside us which stands in opposition to our regular self-image. But the way we get there is messy. To turn such irritations into insight requires an open-minded and challenging process of self-reflection.

It should also be said that Jung's emphasis on seeing our shadow in those who upset us does not mean that there are no truly bad deeds. He did not believe that all badness is just our subjective opinion or an example of moral relativism. He saw evil in the world first-hand – as did all of Europe and much of the

The essential concern for Jung was how we house the Devil inside us – the shadow – and particularly how we do this as a society as a whole with our collective shadow.

world in the twentieth century. He recognized that there was an inner betrayer in us, a part of us that leads us down the worst of all paths. Our personal shadow is the route by which we fall under the spell of collective and archetypal darkness.

THE COLLECTIVE SHADOW

Jung observed that complexes could affect groups of people *en masse*. He saw that certain moments seemed to be expressions of a collective shadow, a bursting forth of a mass psychosis; the repressed side of a whole group coming alive; a tribal Mr Hyde. He saw this madness first-hand in Germany in the 1930s and wrote about it. But every era carries some measure of collective shadow.

One could argue that no moment in time has seen more of the reality of human darkness than ours. Having witnessed the Holocaust and faced the threat of nuclear war in the twentieth century, and now facing the environmental impact of fossil fuels and plastics in the twenty-first century, we are undoubtedly aware of more of humanity's potential for destruction than any of our ancestors ever were. Such a view does not come from a moralizing stance, but is a psychological fact. 'Our era has made forced witnesses of us all.'[25]

The shadow is about where we put the Devil – where do we allow darkness to be housed? Racism and bigotry offer the relief of foisting our group's shadow onto another whom we view as lesser. Doing so enables us to not look at or feel our shadow, and not see our own worst selves. But the collective shadow of our modern culture is also bigger and wider than group-to-group projections. There are culture-wide or civilizational expressions of the collective shadow.

Jung saw the widespread loss of connection to the inner life and to a lived spirituality as one of the primary illnesses of our time. He observed that people were no longer animated by the traditional religions. For more than a hundred years, thinkers and writers, from Nietzsche to F. Scott Fitzgerald, have

The philosopher Friedrich Nietzsche wrote about the so-called 'death of God' and the disappearance of spirituality from the world.

An illustration for Mary Shelley's novel Frankenstein. *Jungian analysts see this as an example of the dangers of the loss of technology's shadow.*

described God as being dead. Church attendance in the West hits new lows with each passing year. For Jung, this meant that we've lost the old way but not yet found the new, and are sitting in a spiritual vacuum.

Into that vacuum, without our awareness, has slipped our fascination with human technology. Observe people closely today and you'll notice that we have an almost magical faith in our devices. People see their computers and phones as all-knowing and expect them to function perfectly all the time, and view pharmaceuticals as magical cure-alls. Where we used to put God, we have now put technology. Where spirit was, we have unconsciously placed human genius.

Because of our tremendous faith in the human creative capacity and in our technology, we have lost any view of its tremendous dark side. Mary Shelley's story of *Frankenstein* illustrates this danger perfectly. (As with Stevenson's tale of the shadow, hers also came to her in a dream.) In the story, a doctor brings a reconstructed dead body back to life, perfectly illustrating how today our former faith in God is now placed firmly into human sciences. Humanity now sees itself as Creator. The Jungian psychotherapist and author Robert Romanyshyn described the lethal nature of this denial in *Victor Frankenstein, the Monster and the Shadows of Technology* (2019). In the bright-sided view of ourselves as Creator, we have lost the shadow of technology as potential destroyer. Jung himself recognized this as the primary danger we face. As he wrote shortly before his death: 'Coming generations will have to take account of this momentous transformation if humanity is not to destroy itself through the might of its own technology and science.'[26]

SEEING YOUR SHADOW

Jung saw the solution to our collective crises in authentic personal work, including the recognition of our shadow. 'The best political, social, and spiritual work we can do is to withdraw the projection of our shadow onto others.' Individuals fall under the spell of mass

A photograph of Carl Jung at his desk in 1953. Jung saw journaling and writing as an important part of honouring the inner life.

psychological psychoses through the particularities of their own personal shadows. Power complexes, for example, might make someone likely to fall into an authoritarian worldview, or greed could lead to doing things people might otherwise never do. Our personal failings are the doorway through which the collective shadow can enter, and therefore they are also the place in which they can be barred. We can avoid entanglement with, reduce our exposure to, and free ourselves from the psychological diseases of our time by effective inner work.

Jung saw as fundamental to this work a practice of establishing an inner relationship to the unconscious. Recording dreams, journaling and psychotherapy develop this inner connection. In his own personal practice, C.G. regularly observed his dreams, drawing many of his inner figures, and painting and even carving others. Both he and other analysts emphasized the importance of bringing the insights from inside into practice in the outer world. Whether it be through art or a change of attitude, respect was to be paid through action. While self-reflection is the missing first step, the relationship with the unconscious ultimately requires our worldly sacrifice. Honouring the voice of the inner life often requires outer deeds: creative work, self-care, taking greater responsibility, better relationships, community service or exercise, for example.

In the next chapter we'll explore what inner work looks like in more detail, but integrating the shadow sometimes begins when we notice ourselves doing something out of character. Perhaps with genuine embarrassment, you wonder: 'Why did I get so angry just then?' For a moment, you're seeing a part of yourself with which you're not very comfortable. Our blind spots are momentarily revealed to us in such ways. Episode 55 of *This Jungian Life*, a podcast hosted by three Jungian analysts, suggests the exercise of written reflection upon someone that you dislike disproportionately as a mirror for generating images of your shadow. Could your reaction suggest something of the rejected part of yourself? The Jungian author Robert A. Johnson tells us that 'the shadow is the part of us we fail to see or know,'[27] and because of this we are most often able to glimpse our shadow only from the ways in which we project it onto others. Consciousness in relationships is usually a key part of day-to-day shadow work. As Prospero says in Shakespeare's *The Tempest*: 'this thing of darkness I/Acknowledge mine.'

Doing work on our shadow almost always opens up the concept of 'family shadow' and patterns of collective and cultural wounding that privilege certain values and ways of being, and reject others. These patterns are carried and ingrained unconsciously. Those playing them out are likely to deny that they are doing so (even to themselves). But we should remember that the ego and the shadow both come about together as a part of our 'civilizing' process. All of us are carrying the tension between the ego and shadow in various forms. The Cartesian division of us from the world is something that we carry in our bodies. It's a common civilizational shadow in our time to have a weakened connection to body, feeling and instinct – many people are 'living in their heads'. How might we be acting out that separation? Jung believed that the only antidote to the crisis of our era was authentic inner work and a return to listening to the voice within us. That search for reconnection usually demands something of us in the real world; a creative sacrifice made in place of neurotic destruction.

HIDDEN TREASURE

Many of us may be able to remember a time before the split. As a three- or four-year-old, we might have memories of being fully enthralled in the moment, completely present in our play. There is a time before the division of ego and shadow within us.

As we grow older, the ego and persona gain form, and the shadow gets tucked away. We're aware of the shadow in moments of conflict, but where does that other side go the rest of the time? The shadow is a structure of character; it is a part of our personality. It is the shadow's threat to the persona which leads to us to ask: 'Who am I?' It is the source of the inner struggle that leads us so often into therapy.

In therapy, we may discover that the shadow is made up not only of repressed drives, 'but also values that consciousness rejects'.[28] No one person can live out all of the great moral values; each of us are better at some and worse at others. If we look closely, we see that people's morality tends to have a shape that celebrates some values and condemns others. Most of us would be surprised to think of ourselves as morally incomplete, but in reality we are one-sided in this way, just as we are in many others. This is why Jung sought to live out the wholeness of who he was, rather than a particular set of virtues. In doing so, we open up a wider ground within us – one with a greater array of responses to life.

The shadow 'does not consist only of morally reprehensible tendencies, but also displays a number of good qualities, such as normal instincts, appropriate reactions, realistic insights, creative impulses, *etc*'.[29] The Jungian analyst David Pressault points out that the shadow can be a vital source within us, one that can 'invite the ego into the places the parental complexes forbid'. Where we might have learned to avoid certain ways of being and have inner voices that reinforce those tendencies, the shadow exists beyond such conditioning – it is a living force within us. Moving past the *thou shalt nots* of our culture may enable us to discover what truly lights us up. Working past inner prohibition may help us to better live out our potential and express our capabilities more fully. Integrating the shadow may help us to live in a way that better accords with what we have inside of us. The shadow is its own entity within us, and as we reconnect it to the light side of ourselves, we often find that we get our energy back. For the shadow 'even contains childish or primitive qualities which would in a way vitalize and embellish human existence, but convention forbids!'[30]

It is also true that there is an 'archetypal shadow' – a quality of darkness which we can never integrate – but we should not let that

It is only by confronting the prohibitions of our culture – as seen in Rembrandt's Moses Smashing the Tablets of the Law *– that we can achieve our potential.*

dismay us too much. As an adult, we are required to face this but not to get caught in it. Confrontation with the archetypal shadow means seeing the reality of evil in the world in broad daylight; not looking away or going immediately into denial (as may happen automatically). But as Nietzsche also warned, we shouldn't look too long at such things for fear of becoming possessed by their character. We'll look at this more in Chapter 5.

We might choose to see our own struggles as a confrontation with the larger darkness in the world. Author and screenwriter Steven Pressfield describes the shadow as Resistance – the force in us that would have us fail rather than succeed. And we can view the shadow in such big, menacing abstract terms. But Jungian analyst Ann Belford Ulanov reminds us that the antidote to the big bad is the little good that each of us can perform: 'Expressed in grand terms, the Devil's trick is to lead us to let go of an evil we can do something about to work for an abstract and idealized good that can never be realized.'[31]

Here, she is pointing out a particular way in which our culture has a predilection for abstraction and for trading our local struggles for big picture dreams. She makes clear another way we can seek to avoid falling prey to the shadow, but this formulation also reminds us of our own place in the world and how it important it us. She emphasizes the sanctity of the good that we can do, and this is a view that Jung shared. Jung saw our struggles with the shadow as part of a larger work of the greatest possible value.

If our journey is successfully navigated, we may feel personally revitalized and re-energized. We may feel a new source of energy flowing within. But that personal alchemy also reflects a larger operation in the world. Jung saw the purpose of consciousness to be healing the divide between light and shadow in the transpersonal sense – a view which reflects the righteousness that we feel about moral action and that sees purposiveness in achieving greater personal consciousness. We'll explore that more near the end of this book.

The shadow is a living part of the personality and therefore wants to be included by us in some form. It cannot be argued out of existence or rationalized into harmlessness. In our efforts to wrestle with it, something new is brought into form, a unity arrives that wasn't present before. In a way that we could never have expected, we're more whole.

Key Points

- **Shadow** – the inner split-off complex that contains our rejected values. The shadow comes into being as a result of ego formation, and contains positive and negative qualities.

- **Persona** – the ideal aspect of ourselves; the way we would like to be seen by others; our false mask of adaptation to society.

- **Projection** – the investment of others with (conscious or unconscious) qualities in ourselves.

- **Collective Shadow** – the rejected qualities of a culture; the unconscious motivating force which can come to possess a group.

CHAPTER 3
Inner Work

WHAT IS INNER WORK?

Jung did not see his psychology as primarily a collection of theories, but rather as an applied practice. Jungian psychology is something that we *do*. Its work is to come into greater relationship with ourselves, to discover and relate to parts of ourselves beyond our regular conscious awareness. Listening to dreams is one definitive example of this practice; in dreams we discover deeper voices living and active inside of us. But there are other ways to do this as well: journaling, creative artwork, active imagination, divination, observation of relationships, analysis and psychotherapy, for example. All of these forms of practice seek to enable us to view the activity of the unconscious in our lives.

Inner work is a form of 'gardening for the mind', according to Jung. Through it, we nurture our psyche and allow it to grow into something greater.

In these forms, inner work seeks to advance what Jung called our 'individuation' – the fulfilment of the blueprint of who we are, including both our conscious and unconscious self. Individuation means becoming more of who we are, less split and less broken inside ourselves; it is the enactment of inner healing. Jung saw his lived process of connecting to the different qualities inside of us as bringing about greater wholeness – healthier internal integration. Being better able to see and accept more of who we are means that there is less internal division between conscious and unconscious. This usually enables us not only to live better, but to relate to others better and to have a clearer view of the world around us. In this way, we can understand inner work as not merely egotistical, self-involved navel-gazing, but as a spiritual quest, a task that we do or fail to do. Effective work with the unconscious heals the split that enabled the ego to come into being.

Jung insisted that: 'To concern ourselves with dreams is a way of reflecting on ourselves . . . Not on the ego but on the self; it recollects that strange self, alien to the ego, which was ours from the beginning, the trunk from which the ego grew. It is alien to us because we have estranged ourselves from it through the aberrations of the conscious mind.'[32]

He saw inner work as a kind of internal gardening, a furthering of the natural process of personal development inside of us. Individuation is the process by which the acorn that we are develops into the oak tree that we could be (and not a donkey – to use the alternative Jung himself offered). We aid or hamper this process (usually predominantly unconsciously) through our attitude towards ourselves, life and the unconscious. To bloom into the fullest possible version of our individual selves requires not only overcoming our personal splits and wounds, but also our familial and social wounding – the ways in which our experiences in life, with our families and world, have impeded our healthy growth. The difficulty of that task makes having help from an objective outsider almost always necessary. But it also requires our honesty with ourselves and our therapist, and a willingness to let go of our current self to make room for something truly new (both of which can be difficult).

The search for who we really are, including both our current known ego self and a future version of ourselves which includes more of our unconscious potential, is the quest of Jungian psychology. In this chapter, we'll look at four main methods of doing that work: dream interpretation, active imagination, shadow integration and Jungian analysis. Jung believed that fulfilling our personal potential, wrestling with our particular demons, finding our way to connect spiritually and living out our fullest self was not only beneficial personally, it was also the route by which we remedy the collective spiritual sickness of our time; it is a pathway to cure the split that lives throughout our culture.

DREAM INTERPRETATION

The interpretation of dreams is humanity's original form of interaction with the unconscious. From the biblical Jacob to the *Epic of Gilgamesh* and throughout our indigenous traditions, we see demonstrations of our ancestors' curiosity about, and respect for, the wisdom of dreams.

The finest inspirations of many of our most revered prophets and most beloved poets came to them while they were asleep. And while it is fashionable in our culture to emphasize the daylight awareness of the waking mind, dreams have a long history of pointing to the future, providing precognitive warning of dangers ahead. In Shakespeare's *Julius Caesar*, his wife Calpurnia warns him of her dream of his imminent death, and while people don't speak of these kind of experiences openly (at a party, say), such dreams are not uncommon in real life. People may not speak of such things freely, but they do tell their therapists and close friends. Those who have dreamt of a tragedy that has come to pass are often left with the guilt of not having done something more to warn people or to prevent those events. But in a world of overly certain believers in materialism, it's hard to come forward as a lone prophet. In Greek myth, Cassandra was cursed to see the future but to never be believed by others, and many people today carry such experiences with them. Jung had awful dreams of rivers of blood, death and destruction throughout 1913 and 1914, which echoed the coming outbreak of World War I; he saw how difficult it is for our culture to accept precognition in dreams.

Freud and Jung came together through their interest in dream interpretation, and disagreements about it would eventually lead to their separation. Freud saw dreams as disguised wishes. Jung, instead, saw them as natural phenomena that spoke inside of us in a symbolic language. It is for this reason that myths and fairy tales are so helpful in understanding dreams; they illustrate the various meanings that a symbol can have. *Amplification* is the term used in Jungian psychology to refer to looking at symbols through their various meanings in mythology. However, using myths to understand dreams does not mean simply equating an inner image with an outer myth. Jung's approach is just the opposite. For Jung, myth is used to open the field of contemplation; it is used with an attitude of not knowing what the dream implies in hopes of finding an answer that evokes a meaningful affective response in the dreamer. Amplification, or the use of myth in interpreting dreams, can sometimes help dreamers to get beyond

their rational armour to the emotional truth present in the dream. Every image has a wide range of symbolic interpretations, a range that is not exhausted by our knowledge but which allows room for as-yet-unknown or even irrational possibilities not yet considered.

An analyst may be curious as to what associations come up for the dreamer in regard to their dream – 'What do those images say to you? What do you imagine the images might refer to?' Such a process has uses, but also limitations. If we go too far into associating, we lose the reality of the dream itself. Immediate personal associations about a dreamer are helpful, but should not be relied upon to discover a dream's meaning.

Jung's first commandment of dream interpretation is that

Palmengruppe am Meer

dreams speak a symbolic language. Myth is used to amplify dream images in search of the meaning that 'clicks' within the dreamer. But Jung's second commandment, so to speak, is the directive not to confuse the map for the territory. No symbol dictionary definition can replace the living landscape that is the dream world; one must start with an attitude of not knowing and not equating one's

A postcard from Carl Jung to Martha Freud from 1907. Jung and Freud were often in contact.

77

Carl Jung dreamt of blood and destruction in 1913 and 1914, which predicted the arrival of World War I.

own particular theory with the dream itself. Thirdly, we are best advised to stick with the dream's exposition, setting and images themselves primarily. Always come back to the actual dream, its action and how it relates to the dreamer's own real life, rather than getting lost on overly fanciful interpretations or overly simplistic theory. Let the dream speak for itself, and return to it patiently. Finally, we should watch for themes from dream series that happen over time.

In the most general terms, dreams are the response of the unconscious to the events of our lives; a description of the inner psychic state of health or illness; or even a warning of things to come. Because Jung viewed the psyche as inherently self-correcting, as having a natural healing function, he saw dreams as very often compensating for an incorrect conscious attitude. Dreams reflect the actual psychological state, including the imbalances of character or attitude possessed by the dreamer. Furthermore, Jung believed the growth of the psyche to be a process of constant back and forth between the conscious and unconscious; we are endlessly unfolding out of our current selves and into a greater version of who we are, which includes parts of us that were previously unconscious. Dreams facilitate this growth, perhaps more so than any other natural function. To the extent that we participate with our dreams, we advance that process within us.

Perhaps what makes dreams so magical to experience is the way they relate to our real lives. To discover real and personal meaning within our dreams is a profound experience, and Jung saw three general ways to discover this meaning. One is to look at dreams on the objective level, where characters and action are taken to refer to people in our real lives. Second, we can view dreams on the subjective level, where each figure is seen to represent something personal within us. Thirdly, a dream can be seen to have meaning on the archetypal level, where we are encountering collective voices within us or meaning intended for the larger world (we'll look more at archetypes in Chapters 4

A letter from Carl Jung to the American physician Smith Ely Jelliffe, explaining the problem of symbols.

and 6). A single dream can be seen as simultaneously having meaning on all three levels.

Today, modern Jungians often describe the space of dreams as having its own reality. Robert Bosnak wrote that a dream 'is not a story, not a movie or test or a theatre play. A dream is a happening in space, an articulation of space. We find ourselves in a space we call "dream" upon awakening.'[33] Dreams have their own reality, and we may feel capable of re-entering a particular dream's space immediately upon waking or sometimes even for days afterwards. Dreams happen in a space that our consciousness goes to while we are not awake. The space that we travel in dreams is the inner natural world, and it is just as real as the world we navigate in physical reality by day.

Typically, we respond to dreams by asking: 'What does this dream mean for me?' Or perhaps: 'Why is the dream happening?' Another approach is to view the dream more relationally and to see it as a living reality that we can engage with ourselves. Dr Stephen Aizenstat, founder of Pacifica Graduate Institute of Santa Barbara, has developed DreamTending™, an approach to dreams that asks us to listen to the dream, to allow it to come forward and open itself to us imaginally – in the world of the imagination, which is just as real as the outer world. In relating to dreams, he suggests that we ask: 'Who is visiting now?' and 'What is happening here?' In addition to association and amplification, he adds animation – treating the dream, its figures and landscapes as though they are alive. We invite them to come forward through our attendance to them.

Of course, the first step in tending to our dreams is to develop a relationship with them by writing them down or recording them. The daily practice of relating to the inner world in this way furthers our relationship to it. We build our connection to the inner life each of us has for ourselves. Jung not only recorded his dreams, but began to paint and carve them too. He spent endless hours depicting their images in ink and paint and wood. Jungians view this part of this process as being very important: as we make the ephemeral into something physical, we honour it. As we concretize the intangible dream image into tangible form, we are doing the one thing it cannot do for itself.

Likewise, Jung also noticed how often the message of dreams was pointing us 'downwards' into the body and the dilemmas of our real lives. Rather than spiritualizing us up and out of the physical world, this healing force within us enlivens us and leads back into relation with it. 'The interpretation of dreams enriches consciousness to such an extent that it relearns the forgotten language of the instincts.'[34] Aizenstat also sees connecting to our animal body as a necessary part of our response to dreams. Too often our rational mind's pursuit of meaning takes us out of the capacity to relate to the living images we encounter in dreams. 'To meet dreams where they live, you must learn to enter the dream and leave your inner analyst behind.'[35]

ACTIVE IMAGINATION

Jung's approach to the unconscious is fundamentally a relational one. In the face of psychological symptoms, he directs us to recognize that something alive within us is speaking. If we are capable of turning off the 'monkey brain' (as the Buddhists call it) and listening quietly inside, those voices that speak to us in symptom will speak to us in image.

Jung called this process *active imagination*. It is begun by believing that the psyche is moving through us on order to try to express itself. If we can listen to the inner images and hold them in our awareness, their story will progress. To serve this process, we should concertize the stories that come. Write them down or, better still, draw or paint them. Build a relationship with the living unconscious inside of us. The process will be blocked if we are caught in the critical mind. It will move forward if we 'let the unconscious take the lead.'[36]

During active imagination, one concentrates on an image or feeling and then 'allows a chain of associated fantasies to develop and gradually take on a dramatic character.'[37] The process is neither simple daydreaming (passive imagination) nor conscious invention, but rather a genuine encounter of conscious awareness with the unconscious inner world.

The first barrier is the doubt of the conscious mind. It can be difficult to accord enough reality to their inner images to enable the dialogue to come to life. Rather than a technique, active imagination is an attitude towards the unconscious, an attitude which takes its reality seriously and allows it to 'live and breathe' on its own. One needs to grant existence to the variety of complexes that move within us. Getting to that acceptance is very difficult because we are used to being identified with our conscious ego and dismissing all other interior voices. Humbert writes, 'censorship and the mechanisms of defence, which lay the foundation for consciousness, confuse, divert and cloud over the dynamic expressions of the unconscious'.[38]

Once you get over your doubt and enter into receptivity, the next step is maintaining this while also consciously engaging with the process yourself. One entertains the guest both with our receptivity and our active company. We listen and then speak, perhaps asking a question or even arguing and pushing back against what we hear said. The action of relating can be an interior fantasy or visualization process, a dialogue or an artistic creation.

Jung turned his relationship with his inner world into innumerable outer-world objects. Drawings, writings, paintings, wood carvings, stone carvings and other items all came into existence through an act of honouring his inner voice. All creative work might be thought to be the product of this inner tension – what does the creative voice spur to be born from you? What does the inner voice whisper?

Active imagination is not a confrontation of ego with the unconscious, but rather a stepping outside of uniformity with the ego's view and entertaining another source within us. It is allowing an Other to be heard with in us – perhaps many Others. Its activity requires holding the tension between our familiar view and the new voice. Holding that tension can bring healing. As a dynamic engagement of consciousness with the unconscious, active imagination can effect a greater inner unity that sticks with us – what Jungians call *wholeness*. It heals by 'using the resources of the unconscious itself to bring dissociated material gradually back into a relationship with the conscious ego'.[39]

Since this is a process that effects actual healing, we might

An illustration of 'The Golden Castle' from The Red Book: Liber Novus *by Carl Jung.*

want to approach the work with reverence. We can see it as being spiritually significant, and active imagination bears a similarity to oracular and shamanistic practices worldwide. Alfred Adler, a Jungian analyst who trained with Jung at the Burghölzli, reminds us that this process draws out an acknowledgement of the unconscious as 'the really potent and creative layer of our psyche . . . it possesses a superior knowledge of our real needs in regard to integration and the ways to achieve them.'

For this same reason, it is generally advised that this process be undertaken only later in analysis, or when we have access to trained professionals or other adept psychological attendants. To enter deeply into the unconscious is a journey of both great healing potential and genuine psychological peril.

SHADOW INTEGRATION

Jung saw in the lives of his patients that there was no one path for everyone: 'The shoe that fits one person pinches another; there is no recipe for living that suits all cases.' He also tended to see psychological value in our mistakes, our bad decisions or errors on the road of life: 'The right way to wholeness is made up, unfortunately, of fateful detours and wrong turnings.' The early community around Jung came to look at worldly blessings as something to be potentially feared for their psychological danger (such as inflation), and to view challenging events in life as something to be celebrated for their great growth potential: 'You're fired? Congratulations!'

Jung saw the shadow as a place of potential value. Our folly can become a source of wisdom if we can face it squarely and see it for what it is. Each person's shadow is different, which makes shadow integration somewhat hard to describe. All of us may have different areas in which we need to grow, or aspects that we need to integrate, but there are general ways of understanding the process.

One of the clinical psychological ways of understanding the shadow is as repressed childhood trauma. Jung often stated that the shadow is our infantile self. In this way, we can understand it as the part of us that is still the most hurt from our earliest experiences. Growing up is almost always a shame-filled experience, and all of us have a split-off self that is primitive. It is for this reason that most people require competent professional psychological help to integrate the shadow.

Because the shadow is constituted from our infantile psychological material, it is often connected to the way in which we relate to our bodies. Most of our first experiences of shame came through our bodies. Thus, for many people, integrating the shadow means healing our relationship to our bodies. Our society is very good at disconnecting us from our bodies; in fact, it has never been better. We are surrounded by screens most of our days, and children are being raised on them. Videos games are everywhere and generate more revenue than films. Consciousness introduced our ability to restrict our instinctual reactions, but that same awareness has now grown into a complete disconnection from our physical selves. All of that involvement with digital representations and abstractions is having an effect on us. We are too much in our heads. Intellectualization is real problem, a way we lose the reality of the world around us. The great Jungian analyst Ann Belford Ulanov describes it this way: 'Post-modern globalization brings many benefits but it also bombards us with so much sensation and information that it is a cause of a kind of promiscuous arousal that knows no anchoring in a specific location, body, society.'[40]

Thus, integrating the shadow for some means digging soundly into their real location, real body, real society. Integrating the shadow today often means changing the way in which we live. It might mean a change in diet, more exercise, a sport, or learning a new sexual trick or two.

The hosts at the podcast of *This Jungian Life* suggested that we look for the shadow in what we like the least, in what bothers us, in what triggers us or disgusts us. In the grip of that reaction, take to paper and pen and write out everything you're feeling. Get curious. What bothers you about it the most? At a bare minimum, you'll be closer to something that's powerful for you.

Jungian analyst and author June Singer noted that active imagination is often a path to shadow work because what it reveals is very often those rejected voices in us: 'Those who have been able to enter successfully into the kind of dialogue know that is something different from suggestion or "seeding the unconscious". The material that comes forth when the controlling tendencies of the ego are suspended is often what is least expected or wanted.'[41]

Considering the process of active imagination in this way might leave us looking at our creative work differently. It is not only fantasy, but the release of something within us that wants to emerge. Fruitful new work is often the by-product of our own inner tensions and offers a relief to them. The work of the artist is not only for the audience, but for the healing of the artist.

Screenwriter Steven Pressfield points to the shadow as Resistance in our creative work. Resistance, he says, is that which prevents us from creating. In his helpful book *The War of Art*, he describes the shadow as that which blocks our potential and living out our best self: 'Most of us have two lives. The life we live, and the unlived life within us. Between the two stands Resistance.' For Jung, the shadow challenges the whole of who we are. There is a force like this that is active within us. While the larger action of nature that we see working the psyche does want awareness to come into being, the shadow wants to remain unconscious. To at least some degree, we want our dark deeds to stay unseen, most of all to ourselves. 'The unconscious wants to become conscious, but just barely.'[42]

In such a dynamic – charged with holding the tension of seeing parts of ourselves that we'd rather not – it is easy to see the relation to addiction. Addiction provides one of the most common experiences of shadow; being unable to control a part of ourselves through conscious will alone is the lived experience of the reality and power of the shadow. The shadow emerges through addiction and expresses itself through it, but there are complicated inner dynamics at play at such times, and these

The author Steven Pressfield takes a Jungian approach when he argues that it is the shadow that prevents creative work.

are often best dealt with by clinical work. Jung also frequently reminded people that one can also be addicted to 'isms', including nationalism and rationalism.

Integrating the shadow means seeing plainly all the ways that we fail, and all the ways that we continue to make the same mistakes over and over again; it means seeing our failings right up close. How many of us want to admit our worst qualities, our weaknesses, our most shameful deeds, our most painful failings? The shadow can be present in our drives for power or living through the inner voices of our mothers or fathers. We might express the shadow through our sexuality, our religiosity or through our financial dealings. We might express it through the way we fail others. Shadow work means wrestling with past regrets and difficult inner realities. Our shadow is the moral dilemmas we are living with, in slow motion.

Jung said: 'This integration cannot take place and be put to a useful purpose unless one can admit the tendencies bound up with the shadow and allow them some measure of realization – tempered, of course, with the necessary criticism. This leads to disobedience and self-disgust, but also to self-reliance without which individuation is unthinkable.'[43]

Facing the shadow, typically at midlife, is one of the most challenging psychological tasks that can be done. It is often begun without our conscious intention, as we begin to see qualities at work in ourselves which we cannot stand and have great difficulty admitting. The shadow is 'the thing a person has no wish to be'. That split-off part of ourselves holds the values we reject and the qualities we don't like to see in ourselves – but, as Jung realized, it wants to become more integrated into our awareness. In the process, something unexpected happens.

For Jungians, the personal shadow is also a life-bringing figure. Integrating the shadow means plugging into lost sources of energy and inspiration. It is a loosening up of unnecessary rigidities inside us and a broadening of our attitude towards life. It usually means a stronger lived connection to an inner spiritual centre; it often means the achievement of greater faith, strong empathy for others and for our future self. June Singer described the real change that occurs when shadow integration is successful: 'Narrow attitudes become broadened, one-sidedness gives way to the capacity to view a situation from several positions, aggression is replaced by productive activity and passivity becomes receptivity. The changes are often subtle, but they go deep, and people who experience them know that they are living a different way than they did before.'[44]

Shadow work is bringing something home inside us. In service of that reunion, it is good to characterize our shadow as a living 'other' inside us; one who possesses qualities that we reject and hate in ourselves. We can feel that personal shadow living inside us and to relate to it: 'To become conscious of it involves recognizing the dark aspect of the personality as present and real.' Becca Tarnas, a scholar of both Carl Jung and J.R.R. Tolkien, observed how well Tolkien's character of Gollum exemplifies this figure inside of us: 'Nearly every analysis recognizes how the creature Gollum resembles the Shadow, identifying him either as Frodo's personal Shadow, or the collective Shadow figure for the three hobbits Frodo, Sam, and Bilbo. I would add that Gollum is also the personification of his own Shadow, in that Gollum is a distinct personality that has split off from the original personality of the hobbit Sméagol.'[45]

Hearing the voice of the shadow brings discomfort; it is our inner opposite, something with which we will always disagree. Although connection to it and even a healthy integration is possible, we never settle into an accord with it. Throughout Tolkien's *The Hobbit* and *The Lord of the Rings*, the protagonists of Bilbo and Frodo maintain a relationship to the split-off shadow figure of Gollum. They resist the desire to kill Gollum, and his partnership with them contributes to the successful resolution of their quests. Similarly, Jungian analyst Elisabeth Pomès described the evolution of the process with her personal shadow this way: 'I felt at first that acceptance [of the shadow]

The creature Gollum from J.R.R. Tolkien's The Lord of the Rings *can be interpreted as Frodo's shadow.*

meant agreeing with those parts of myself. Gradually I came to realize that it was not the case: accepting and recognizing meant making those aspects of myself conscious. It did not mean necessarily liking them or condoning them but accepting that they were there.'[46]

JUNGIAN ANALYSIS

Jungian Analysis is a psychotherapeutic approach which seeks to establish a more healthy integration of the conscious and unconscious. The outcome of this work is wholeness, a fuller accommodation of the unconscious into our lived experience and a greater fulfillment of who we truly are – individuation. That work effects the relief from psychological symptoms, improved metal health and the maturation of the personality. It usually also brings with it the discovery of personal meaning and a deepened personal spirituality.

A Jungian analyst is someone who leads individuals through this process. Analysts are trained at Jung Institutes worldwide, and those who undertake this training are typically over 40 years of age and usually have a graduate university degree. Candidates for training must also have completed 100 hours of personal work with a Jungian analyst before beginning. Once they are accepted into the training programme, they must complete approximately another 350 hours of their own personal work. While the training of Jungian analysts also includes a tremendous amount of clinical work and academic education, on a par with most clinical psychological doctoral programmes, its emphasis is upon wrestling with one's own material, and that makes Jungian analysts different from other psychologists.

People who are drawn to Jungian psychology often enter therapy with an eye towards its grand archetypal vistas, but most often the psychological work begins with attending to the muck of early life pain and trauma and the bolstering of the personal ego.

Nearly every client, or *analysand* as they are called in Jungian analysis, has some form of early childhood trauma. Jung saw much of that material as contributing to one's personal shadow, and Jungian analysts are trained not only to look for those connections but to understand how early life trauma affects us psychologically. Studies in attachment theory and other schools of modern psychological thought are part of the training of today's Jungian analysts.

Prior to integrating the contents of the unconscious, most analysands must first shore up their personal ego. In this case, the therapist will work to reinforce the positive parts of the personality and help the client to recognize their own capacities and good qualities. The genuine relationship between the analyst and analysand is one of the ways by which the ego grows into greater health. The personally related stance of the analyst towards the client is one of the key differences between the Jungian and Freudian approaches. Rather than assuming a pose of reserved objectivity or cool distance, Jungian therapists invest themselves openly in their clients. They are transparent about their empathy for them and welcome discussions of variations in how each party is feeling about the other. Part of what is happening in Jungian therapy is the development of a genuine relationship between analyst and client. One of the products of that relationship is a healthier ego in the client.

Once the sturdiness of the ego is established, work at facing the unconscious can begin. Jungian psychology is built upon the observation that the effects of the unconscious cannot be overcome by the power of the will. 'Depth psychology integrates itself into the confrontation between conscious and unconscious. [It is an attempt to] understand the mechanisms that govern these interactions.'[47] A Jungian analyst is someone who has learned first-hand how to successfully navigate the unconscious forces within them. As you turn to face the unconscious, you're being met by a guide who has walked the territory you are now walking. Not only should a good analyst have done their work, they should be continuing to do it. The integration of the unconscious is a lifelong, ongoing work.

A good therapist is someone who continues to grow in their awareness of the dynamic activity of complexes within us. They continue to try catch glimpses of their own blind spots and work with a supervisor or analyst themselves in order to get help. Both through their rigorous clinical education and through their own continuing encounter with the unconscious, Jungian analysts know the plumbing of the psyche.

An analyst will be able to help differentiate between the parental complexes, which you might be experiencing as critical voices inside you, and the shadow, which might be coming out in the route you use to stop listening to those critical voices. An analyst knows that people who live through their persona too much are in danger of losing their real individuality. An analyst knows to look for the unlived life of the parent that has been foisted onto the undesiring child.

Psychotherapy always has to do with the whole of our lives, particularly our relationships. Jungian analysis is not just about looking at dream interpretation and at our spontaneous fantasies too; it's about the areas that get the most attention which get neglected. Perhaps most of all, it's not just about insight, it's about doing something with it. It's about living more fully, finding what needs to be lived out by us and doing it. Morally witnessing someone's life so closely demands that we participate with them, that we ask them to live out what is possible for them, what is healthy for them, what is necessary for them.

Toni Wolff exemplified this perhaps more than anyone. The bestselling Jungian author Robert A. Johnson tells the story of how she would insist that her analysands followed the insight that had come to them from the unconscious: 'And what did you do about your dream last week?' Wolff felt strongly that one of the reasons for analysis proving unsuccessful was that people refused to actually do what was asked of them by their dreams and by their lives. It was too easy to stay up in our heads in the realm of ideas. What the psyche wants and what we need is to bring that insight into our living bodies.

Toni Wolff (1888–1953) was a leading Jungian analyst who had a close relationship with Carl Jung.

Wolff emphasized the importance of doing something tangible in the real world from the insight we gained. Without it, healing couldn't take place. In living it out, our attitude towards life changed and grew: 'Patients who had done something specific, something concrete and physical were safe from the wrath to come. But if they hemmed and hawed, or said they thought about it a little, or talked with someone about it, or some such vague thing, she would turn them around and steer them back through the door. As the door was slamming behind them, she would say: "Come back when you mean business."[48]

Key Points

- **Individuation** – the fulfilment of the blueprint of who we are, including both our conscious and unconscious self.

- **Wholeness** – the state of increased integration of unconscious material into consciousness. The goal of analysis, wholeness is often defined in contradistinction from perfection.

- **Symbolic Language** – Jung observed that the unconscious speaks in the language of symbol. An image is to be understood as having a spectrum of possible meanings, which are related through a meaningful theme.

- **Association** – the related notions that come to mind in regard to a symbolic content; the spontaneous ideas that occur around a dream image.

- **Amplification** – the multiplying of understanding of a symbol through looking at its various meanings in mythology.

- **Active Imagination** – a process of cultivation of an inner space in which imagery comes to life and conscious dialogue with inner figures is made possible.

- **Analysis** – a form of psychotherapy that seeks to bring unconscious contents into awareness.

- **Jungian Analyst** – a graduate of the training programme from a Jung Institute. Jungian analysts complete extensive inner personal exploration and psychological clinical training.

- **Analysand** – a participant in Jungian analysis (the client).

CHAPTER 4
The Self

WHAT IS THE SELF?

Perhaps the most primary concept in Jung's psychology is that of the Self. Jung believed that there was a central force guiding our development: he saw this energy expressed in our ability to change form and evolve, while maintaining our personal identity. As with the nautilus, whose shell repeats its spiral form while growing larger, nature preserves our inherent pattern while spurring our transformation. There is an instinct within living systems to endlessly renew themselves while maintaining the integrity of their unique structure. In our personal lives, the Self is the blueprint of our potential unfolding and the path to greater unity of the conscious and unconscious in us. Jung saw it perpetually reorienting us towards balance and guiding us into greater wholeness. Like many of nature's systems, the psyche is self-regulating.

The nautilus shell has a pattern that repeats itself while growing ever larger, just as we ourselves have a pattern that is preserved even as it grows.

Jung believed that the 'growth of the personality comes out of the unconscious.'[49] The personal Self is the drive to fulfil our own particular unfolding and become who we are. Individuation is a process that wants to bring the conscious and unconscious into optimal relation with each other. Attending to what the unconscious is trying to bring to the table in that exchange is the work of Jungian psychology. Whether we attend to it through dreams or do other inner work (or don't), we may come to discover the unconscious operating in the conflicts of real life. Certainly by midlife (if not sooner), many people are seeing their own irrational behaviour or other clues that point to something beyond the ego at work within themselves. A symbolic appreciation of the dilemmas of our daily lives is difficult to achieve, but it provides an eye for what's unfolding within us from underneath. One way or another, serving the interchange between conscious and unconscious is what ensures that we grow into what we are meant to be. It is in this way that the 'acorn becomes an oak and not a donkey!' The alternative – growth of our conscious self without connection to the unconscious – tends to make people rigid, unadaptable and ultimately unhappy. The extent to which we relate to our inner world is the extent that there is likely to be reduced conflict within us. Inner work can change our attitude about the outer world. We are more at ease when we are not odds with ourselves. This sympathy of action and inner state is related to the Chinese Tao. In becoming more whole, we become more of who we are, and we usually become better able to express ourselves and share our particular gifts. In listening deeply inside, we may feel closer to the inner centre. Finding meaning in the growth patterns of our lives weaves us into the world more deeply and more dynamically.

For Jung, the Self is the source of our drive to individuate and of our innate spiritual and moral impetus. Experiences of the Self are numinous, powerful, moving and transcendent. Alongside our powerful biological instincts stands an equally powerful urge to become who we could be and to connect to something beyond the personal.

The Chinese character for 'Tao'. Carl Jung's approach was significantly influenced by Taoism.

In witnessing the Self spurring our growth, Jung also glimpsed a containing force within the psyche, a larger frame holding the tension between conscious and unconscious, and the dynamic interplay between them. For Freud, consciousness represses certain experiences, forcing them down in the unconscious. For Jung, the unconscious is the ground out of which consciousness itself emerges.

The Self is Jung's answer to the following question: What in us makes us strive to be more aware, more conscious, more moral, more loving, more embodied, more whole? Religious beliefs most often put God at the centre of that drive in us, and Jung saw an overlap between our images of the Self and our images of God. As it expresses the unity of the whole psyche, the Self is connected to our images of the divine.

At the top of the psychological hierarchy, Freud put the Superego – our personal intake of the collective civilizing influence present around us; the moral force of previous generations, which we experience in our upbringing. For Freud, humanity itself is the source of our drive to greater moral and psychological understanding.

IMAGES OF THE SELF

Jung saw a compulsion towards creating centred or circular images in the psyche, both in times of breakdown and at times of heightened awareness. When a patient has hit rock bottom and is in a full crisis or has lost their sense of who they are, Jung noticed that they may draw circles or other images of a centred boundary, a reflection of the need for the return of order and structure. Also, if we look at our sacred images, images of religious contemplation such as the mandala image, both Eastern and Western, we find this same expression of four-square, balanced, concentric and enclosed designs.

A primary image of the Self is the *temenos* or magic circle. Here, we see the Self as protective. In many indigenous traditions, the spiritually ill person is placed into a physically constructed sacred circle and is healed there through being led to reconnecting to the centre inside themselves. Jung observed that when 'there is a great disorder and chaos in a man's mind, this symbol can appear in the form of a mandala in a dream'[50] or in his spontaneous drawings. *Mandala* is a term from Sanskrit meaning magic circle, and Jung saw these patterns as a vehicle for psychic movement. The appearance of the images of the Self remind us that the centre of the psyche does exist, that there is an order-making, containing field present and available to us within. These images are traditionally used for religious devotion, and our images of the Self overlap with our images of the divine. June Singer noted that 'the circle or sphere seems best to give shape to the ideas of the Self's centrality, its extensity and its encompassing character.'[51] She also powerfully described the Self as that 'which in some mysterious way a person must penetrate with their creative potential.'[52] Ann Ulanov has said that the Self is the way we know God.

As children, our parents may be image-holders of the archetypal Self. We project our containing capacity onto them, and parents can hold the place of Gods within us. This may live with us as adults still, and shape how we unconsciously feel about the world. As the personal Self is our own drive to individuation, therapy often involves the exploration of the gap between our Self and the way our parents held that image for us or failed to do so. One can imagine the role a guru could take in that conflict as well, becoming a new vehicle for the projection of the Self.

In Jung's own personal psychological work, images of the Self were a key. As noted by Jung's family members in their commentary upon his art, 'The mandala motif is the most depicted figure in *The Red Book*.'[53] Throughout the world of sacred art, images of the Self are everywhere: picture the Chartres labyrinth, the (still surviving) rose window of Notre Dame in Paris, beautiful Navajo or Tibetan sand paintings, or the cosmic diagrams of the alchemists.

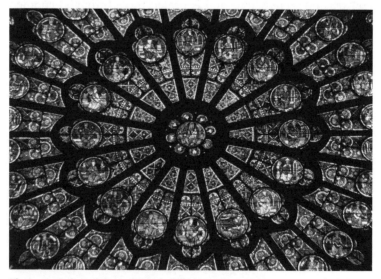

The rose window of the cathedral of Notre Dame in Paris is a piece of religious art that depicts the Self through the motif of a mandala.

In Jung's book on UFOs,[54] he focused on the relationship of flying saucers to the Self. Their circularity and numinous quality made them ideal vehicles for the projection of our inner centre. I look at this correlation in regard to crop circles (mysteriously formed patterns in grain fields) in my own 2014 book.[55] The placement of those images in living crops speaks to the nature of the Self as not only upwards into the spiritual, abstract and the mental, but also into the body, the world and nature. The Jungian analyst and author Lionel Corbett has emphasized that the Self can also appear in natural or biological forms, including plants and animals. Such an appearance often suggests the need for the dreamer to reconnect with their physical or instinctual selves.[56]

Jung saw a specific emphasis upon the Self in our civilization. 'And do you know what the Self is for Western man? It is Christ, for Christ is the archetype of the hero, representing man's highest aspirations. All this is very mysterious and at times frightening.'[57] Perhaps what was so frightening about the formulation of the Self that he was describing in us is that it is an extraordinarily one-sided character – one that only sees itself in the light of its own highest aspirations and thus misses its shadow entirely. Is this shadow being reflected back to us today in tragic form by the effects of climate change and by discordant political figures? Are we being led to see the missing ugly side of our dominant character?

For more on the archetypal Self, please check out Jeffrey Miller's *The Transcendent Function*, Jung's *Symbols of Transformation*, Lionel Corbett's *The Religious Function of the Psyche*, *Archetype Revisited* by Anthony Stevens, *Ego and Archetype* by Edward F. Edinger, and *Self and Liberation: The Jung/Buddhism Dialogue* by Daniel J. Meckel and Robert L. Moore.

JUNG VERSUS FREUD

In 1906, Jung published his work in the Word Association Experiment. Freud read *Diagnostic Association Studies* that same year, and the two men began an intense correspondence that lasted for years. Theirs was a potent relationship.

A group portrait including Sigmund Freud (bottom row, left) and Carl Jung (bottom row, right) during a visit to Clark University, Massachusetts in 1909.

Jung had already been a student of Freud's work from afar, and in 1908 he became editor of the newly founded professional journal *Yearbook for Psychoanalytical and Psychopathological Research*. In 1909, they travelled together for the Clark

A letter from Sigmund Freud to Carl Jung, 3 January 1913, which marked the end of the close friendship between the two analysts.

University lectures, which helped to legitimize psychoanalysis in the United States. During their long sea journey, they analyzed each other's dreams.

In 1910, Freud proclaimed his intention that Jung be his professional successor. Jung did become president of their professional association, but for a long time the heir apparent had been having doubts about some of his teacher's views. In 1912, Jung published *Psychology of the Unconscious*, in which he publicly made clear his serious philosophical differences with Freud.

Freud's theory maintained that the primary source of inner conflict was repressed sexuality. Jung believed that personal development was a calling of its own within the psyche. Freud saw psychology as entirely personal and biological; Jung saw in his patients and in himself a level of the unconscious beyond the personal. Freud believed that not only neurosis but also all creativity and religiosity were expressions of repressed instinct; Jung saw human nature as having a profoundly deep spiritual instinct. Freud saw unconscious images as relating to specific historic causal factors; Jung saw them as symbolic, and having a range of possible archetypal expressions, including irrational possibilities. Freud saw the inner life as reducible to biological urges; Jung saw transpersonal patterns emerging in the dreams of his patients. At this time, Freud was tremendously resistant to all spiritual possibilities – and Jung thought he understood why.

Freud's grandfather Schlomo had been a Hasidic Jewish Rabbi, and Sigmund rejected both his grandfather's mysticism and religion in general. Jung's innate philosophical milieu was one in which spirituality and religion were intertwined; he had grown up with mediumistic relatives, and his father and uncles were all priests. While Jung had experienced first-hand the shadow side of those forms, he also had no psychological need to split one from the other. Throughout his life, he and his family also experienced paranormal events, which Jung included in his understanding of the world.

Jung grew from the psychological benefits of his father-son relationship with Freud, and spoke with respect of the importance of his pioneering work throughout his life. But with *Psychology of the Unconscious*, later called *Symbols of Transformation*, his break with Freud was made public.

In November 1912, at a meeting in Munich, Jung disagreed with Freud's interpretation of an Egyptian symbol, eventually connecting the dialogue to disagreements in the larger psycho-analytic movement. Freud fainted and Jung carried him to a couch. At the Fourth International Psychoanalytical Congress in September 1913, Jung lectured on his work on Psychological Types. It was the last time that Freud and Jung saw each other.

Carl Jung (right) discusses an Egyptian sculpture with Dr Carleton Smith in 1955.

CONFRONTATION WITH THE UNCONSCIOUS

Following the loss of his relationship with Freud, Jung admitted to feeling disoriented. A powerful, influential mentor had provided a tremendously stabilizing influence for him, and now he was a man on his own. He proposed to meet his clients with a dogma-free approach that allowed the unconscious to speak for itself as much as possible; to trust the associations his patients made with their dreams, and whatever sparked from their mutual dialogue. This natural approach to working with the unconscious was satisfying for him, giving stability to his work and bringing with it a feeling of peace.

In the autumn of 1913, however, Jung began to feel a deep unease. In October, he had a horrifying vision of bloody carnage across Europe. The vision came a second time – and demanded to be recognized consciously by him. He felt that he might be having a psychosis. At the outbreak of World War I, however, he accepted that the psyche has a fateful quality and is capable of preceding the ego in space and time.

Jung had to admit there was wisdom in the psyche, and he was then tasked with listening to it. He pushed himself to overcome his own disbelief in the process and to sit with uncomfortable emotions and with his inner figures, feelings and images. He entered into fantasies, and when an inner character arose, he inquired as to their message. He 'made it a rule never to let a figure or figures that he encountered leave until they had told him why they had appeared to him'.[58] He dedicated himself to recording the exchanges and illustrating what he saw in them and in his dreams.

He began to use his hands to bring his inner images into the outer world. He crafted his experiences of the unconscious into material form. Over his lifetime, he carved wooden figures and bas reliefs, made freestanding stone sculptures and painted wall paintings and ceiling murals – all inspired by his inner life. In the period from the end of 1913 until 1917, he put particular dedication into a series of primary manuscripts. He would then

An illustration from The Red Book: Liber Novus *by Carl Jung.*

spend until 1930 turning those dialogues into a beautifully bound manuscript, a facsimile of which was published in 2009 as *The Red Book: Liber Novus*. Using calligraphic pen, multicoloured ink and gouache paint, the book contains millions of individually painted cells and handwritten text. The work brings his most powerful encounters with the unconscious to life. It is a stunning testament to Jung's devotion to his unconscious.

Jung listened to the voices from the unconscious and took what they said seriously, regardless of the judgements of his conscious mind. Then he used the process of making art to allow his hands to unfold what the ego resisted – and discovered the power of creativity as healing work.

With an attitude of play, Jung held the tension between the emergent inner voice and the ego. Out of the well-held inner dialogue, something new emerges: a new understanding, a new attitude or a symbol. Jung called this the *transcendent function*. 'As I worked with my fantasies, I became aware that the unconscious undergoes or produces change.'[59] This process works especially between the ego and shadow. But the ego must let go of needing to control the outcome. 'The ego must renounce all attempts to appropriate unconscious dynamics.' Doing so 'allows libido to regress into the unconscious and thereby makes it possible for new forms to emerge.'[60]

In *Memories, Dreams, Reflections*, Jung tells the story of a dream of an emerald green table around which sat his children. A dove descended and soon after transformed into a young girl with golden blonde hair. She played with his children and put her arm around him, and before departing as the dove again, left him a message. The dream eventually led Jung to a potent memory of a childhood emotion of feeling enraptured while playing with his blocks. He realized that this part of him still lived on: 'The small boy is still around, and possesses a creative life which I lack.' Not only was this energy alive in him, it offered a renewal of the creative function in him if he could honour it and make room for it in his life, in his psyche, in his attitude.

For the rest of his life, Jung tried to enact that call to play in specific, rejuvenating ways. The possibility of relating to an inner figure and living out what it asks of us is one of the qualities of maturity in the Jungian view. Jung himself regarded the inner figures as having their own source of consciousness, their own reality, and as offering something to the conscious mind that it could not receive any other way.

Throughout this period of time, Jung sometimes feared for his sanity. He pushed on for his own sake and the sake of his patients, and this depth of inner work was the basis upon which his psychology was built. Luckily, he had his wife Emma and children to ground him in reality, and Toni Wolff as his partner in the inner journey. Wolff, too, was trapped in his descent, but she most certainly contributed to his successful emergence out of this period. Emma Jung said, 'I shall always be grateful to Toni for doing for my husband what I or anyone else could not have done at a most critical time.'[61]

While Jung's creative acts in service of the unconscious brought the inner life out into the world, he also had a great deal of reckoning to do in the outer world. One of the chapters in *Symbols of Transformation* was entitled 'The Sacrifice', and

Carl Jung with his wife Emma. She helped to keep him level-headed while he pursued his inner work.

Jung knew that this book meant the loss of Freud for him. He recognized the necessity of the loss of the object of projection and the reclamation of the energy it contained. Coming into adulthood meant relinquishing the desire for unconscious, childlike bliss and letting go of regressive fantasies. Looking squarely at ourselves often meant seeing things we didn't want to see and recognizing the damage that we're doing. 'The man who recognizes his shadow knows very well that he is not harmless.'[62] Jung had grown through a Father projection on Freud, but now he would have to find that energy inside himself. While his confrontation with the unconscious had cost him his friendship with Freud, it had nevertheless provided him something very tangible inside of himself.

He would later reflect:

> In myths the hero is the one who conquers the dragon, not the one who is devoured by it. And yet both have to deal with the same dragon. Also, he is no hero who never met the dragon, or who, if once he saw it, declared afterwards that he saw nothing. Equally, only one who has risked the fight with the dragon and is not overcome by it wins the hoard, the 'treasure hard to attain'. He alone has a genuine claim to self-confidence, for he has faced the dark ground of his self and thereby has gained himself. This experience gives some faith and trust, the [faith] in the ability of the self to sustain him, for everything that menaced him from inside he has made his own. He has acquired the right to believe that he will be able to overcome all future threats by the same means. He has arrived at an inner certainty which makes him capable of self-reliance.[63]

INDIVIDUALITY AND COLLECTIVITY

From the horrors of World War I to the rise of the Nazis, Jung saw first-hand what happens when societies descend into mass psychosis. Rather than being an insulation against evil, Jung saw that cultures could inspire it. In large groups, the psyche can be brought down to the lowest common denominator, for it is to this

Jung used the metaphor of a hero battling a dragon to demonstrate how it is only by facing the dark side of our self that we can achieve self-reliance.

lowest level that everyone in the group can genuinely connect. While nationhood (or any other group identity) offers belonging, unity, shared values and shared purpose, there is a dark side to the herd that lives inside of us. Culture generally serves the function of reforming our instincts in favour of moral action, but it can also normalize behaviour that serves our lowest instincts and our worst selves. A desire to belong to one's tribe can lead people to perform horrific deeds. An unconscious allegiance to authority can lead one to take part in atrocities. The drive to serve the tribe without question is also a part of who we are. For these reasons, Jung felt that institutions should be regarded sceptically.

People will take on the spirit of the group and become identified with it, especially if they identify the group with their persona. The persona-oriented individual is especially keen on saving face publicly and being seen in a good light. When the ego identifies with the persona, 'the subject's centre of gravity lies in the unconscious. It is then practically identical with the collective unconscious, because the whole personality is collective. In these cases . . . the destruction of conscious ideals is feared.'[64] Here, the tribal vision provides strength and identity, and change will not be welcomed.

Without a conscious connection to the process of individuation, we tend to project the inner figures outwards onto religions, causes, philosophies and ideas that then hold a fascination for us for a period of time – until we're disillusioned and start over again with a new object. In this way, business or political causes can take on a religious fervour or a particular person becomes wondrous for a while for us, and then the 'dreamboat turns out to be a footnote'. While both love and faith have tremendous positive qualities, there are occasions where we use those vehicles to resolve something unsettled in ourselves. We find a comforting

For Jung, Nazism represented a mass psychosis and demonstrated the potential dangers that culture could present.

oversimplification to believe in, and it soothes us for a period of time. Without conscious reflection, we're still worshipping the ancient gods of war and love, but we're doing it in the form of politics or consumerism.

Jung saw people fall under the grip of the collective shadow through their own personal shadows. If people were greedy, that was how they compromised their way under its spell. Our weaknesses and our neuroses open the door to fall into the mass psychoses of our times. Likewise, our successful inner work can close the door. Achieving a stable sense of self in connection to our inner life and a psychic adaptability and flexibility will allow us to bend without breaking when the dark winds blow. If we have truly faced our own shadow and resisted it, we find it easier to act morally under the pressure of the real world. Relating to our inner selves, accepting and loving who we are in our fullness strengthens our character. Marie-Louise von Franz, one of the greatest of Jungian analysts and authors, wrote that individuation makes one 'capable of choosing its own path and self-reliantly remains true to its own inner law. Especially in times of collective neurosis, the existence of such mature people is of crucial importance.'[65]

While Jung believed strongly in the necessity of understanding ourselves in relation to parents and ancestors, he also believed that individuation compels 'a progressive differentiation from the collective psyche'.[66] The urge towards tribal belonging opposes the urge for individuation. There is a tremendous unconscious pull in societies to go along to get along; to conform; to be like everyone else; to share and live by collective values. A collective attitude 'is dangerous because it is very apt to check and smother all personal differentiation'.[67] Social norms often reinforce a rejection of independent thinking; being different may mean being ousted. People experience a conflict between who they really want to be and who others expect them to be. 'Individuality and collectivity . . . are related by guilt.'[68]

Key Points

- **The Self** – the quality of self-regulation within us, the Self is the archetype that drives us towards healthy balance, greater growth and wholeness and further individuation. This part of us encompasses both our consciousness and the unconscious, and is often symbolized in images of unity.

- **Images of the Self** – these include centred designs and circles, most prototypically the mandala.

- **The Transcendent Function** – a psychological process which enables our growth and individuation. When we are able to hold the tension between two opposite positions, a third new possibility is often brought into being. This brings healing by overcoming one-sidedness in consciousness.

- **Confrontation with the Unconscious** – beginning with disturbing images that presaged the upcoming World War I, during this period of Jung's life he was overwhelmed by images of the unconscious. Working through this time led him to discover much of his psychology, including the practice of active imagination.

CHAPTER 5
Personality Types

DESCRIBING PERSONALITY

Jung believed that each of us is a particular seed, planted in a particular moment into a specific biological and cultural setting. That setting brings with it historic and familial traumas that damage us, as well as blessings that heal us and help us grow. We are also living with the effects of trauma and blessing upon previous generations. Jung felt that it was vital to our psychological health that we regain our sense of being rooted physically, historically, psychologically and spiritually. He knew the necessity of therapeutically facing all of that, including the unlived lives of our parents that are often foisted onto us.

Jung saw people as unique, but he did not believe that we come into the world as blank slates. He believed that we have certain constitutional predispositions that form who we are. He did not think that it is our context alone which creates human personality; a part of our philosophy of life is present at birth and exists prior to the influence of parents and society. This can include the kind of one-sidedness that allows for exceptional performance but leaves us imbalanced. For example, some children show signs of athletic prowess from an early age; they endlessly drive to move, climb and go, and have an innate facility

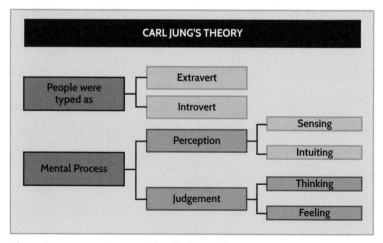

The various personality types identified by Carl Jung.

for the kinetic. We tend to be gifted in some fields of endeavour and limited in others. Jung believed that there are qualities in our character which are essential.

In 1921, Carl Jung published *Psychological Types*, introducing the world to the terms *Extravert* and *Introvert*. The work was the product of two decades of study of human personality. Jung admitted that in writing it he drew not only upon his clinical experience but from his personal life, including both 'friend and foe'. It is a study of how consciousness works in practice, how some of us naturally perceive and respond to the world differently. It is a look at the reality of how people diverge in what gives them energy and how they make judgements. *Psychological Types* proposed two differing primary attitudes: Extraversion and Introversion – Extraverts get energy from interacting with others, while Introverts restore their energy from downtime alone. It also proposed four functions: Sensation and Intuition – ways by which we perceive the world; and Thinking and Feeling – ways by which we make value judgements. His construction of these polarities was also drawn from his observation of the differing schools of thought of Sigmund Freud and another of Freud's protégés, Alfred Adler.

Jung saw Freud's theory as representing an extraverted orientation and Adler's an introverted one. He saw their diverging psychological opinions as stemming from their opposing ways of seeing the world. In this way, Jung's exploration of personality begins from this first binary opposition. Jung puts a great many elements of character into this first division, and over time he peels more binaries apart to provide greater clarity into personality.

His correspondence reveals that, at first, Jung combined Extraversion and Feeling (making it easier to see the connection with Freud's instinct-based theory), and Introversion and Thinking (in parallel with Adler's reflective ego-oriented psychology). With time, Jung learned to differentiate this 'clump' of character traits into finer and more accurate oppositions.

Jung came to see Thinking and Feeling as its own category, defined by opposing ways of evaluating the world. Thinkers value

Alfred Adler (left) with the German neurologist Leonhard Seif. Jung saw Adler's theories as reflecting an introverted approach to the world.

objectively – what's fair is treating everyone the same way. Feelers value subjectively – what's fair is treating each case individually. 'It is one's psychological type which from the outset determines and limits a person's judgement.'[69]

It is believed by some that Toni Wolff contributed to *Psychological Types* by proposing the opposition between Sensate and Intuitive types. It is easy to recognize why: Wolff herself embodied the Intuitive – reading between the lines all the time and knowing through the unconscious (irrational function). Jung's wife Emma embodied the Sensate type – a keen appreciation for detail and knowing through conscious awareness (rational function). The Sensate perceives each tree in a forest with acuity; the Intuitive sees the forest swaying. With this addition, and perhaps with Wolff's help, Jung's understanding of personality unfolded one dimension further.

The process of accurately describing human personality for Jung began with the single division between Extravert and Introvert, and was refined further over time. This process continues today through the study of what is called Personality Type – a more generic term for the study of character around these forms, including approaches that came after Jung.

EXTRAVERTS AND INTROVERTS

Extravert means outward-turning, and *Introvert* means inward-turning. These attitudes, as they are called, describe the way in which our psychic energy moves naturally, either towards the outer world or towards the inner. In common usage today, Extravert refers to someone who is outgoing and talkative – energized through social engagement; while Introvert, generally speaking, refers to someone who is withdrawn or quiet socially, and social engagement may tire them out. The Extravert's energy goes to objects (people and things) of the outer world; the Introvert's energy goes to the inner world. Both are seen as healthy ways of operating; for Jung, both approaches are normal. We all have some energy going to both, but have a dominant preference.

Katharine Cook Briggs and her daughter Isabel Briggs Myers used Psychological Types to develop the Myers-Briggs Type Indicator (MBTI™) – a psychological instrument used to help identify how best to utilize women who were coming into the industrial workforce during World War II. Studies of results from the MBTI™ generally described the ratio of Introverts to Extraverts as 1:1 (evenly split), or in some populations 6:4. In her book *Quiet: The Power of Introverts in a World That Can't Stop Talking*, Susan Caine found that 33–50% of the American population are Introverts.

The Extravert is gregarious: the classic example is the comedian who is more and more energized from the crowd as the evening's performance goes on. They come off stage and are lit for a long time afterwards; they crave stimulation to calm down. The Introvert restores through downtime and quiet. Jung was the classic Introvert. His attention was clearly naturally drawn inwards (as was Adler's). Concentration is on outer objects for Extraverts, and on inner ones for Introverts.

Biological studies show that there are types of people for whom external stimulation is calming and others for whom too much external stimulation is overwhelming. Smoking, coffee and other stimulants tend to soothe Extraverts. Notice for yourself whether you see outgoing people getting calmed by stimulation. Introverts often find stimulants overwhelming. That biological division would seem to echo the physiological existence of Jung's Introvert–Extravert category.

Introvert and Extravert represent types of characteristic structuring of consciousness. But 'these attitudes are not meant to characterize behaviour. One can meet contemplative monks who are extravert and businessmen who are introverted.'[70] All of us can display times of introversion and extraversion, but as types, this basic division is one of the easiest for us to see.

Introvert and *Extravert* are terms that have a well-recognized understanding in our world today. Virtually every comprehensive model of personality has some category similar to it. However, when we look closely at how Jung used those terms, there seem to be several different aspects merged into one. The Extraverts are energized by the outer world, socially oriented and not reflective; the Introverts are introspective, socially averse and get energy from time alone. Are individuals always these three together?

Jung writes that the Introvert 'has no love of enthusiastic get-togethers. He is not a good mixer. What he does, he does in his own way, barricading himself against influences from outside … His own world is a safe harbour, a carefully tended and walled-in garden, closed to the public and hidden from prying eyes. His own company is the best.'[71] Undoubtedly, we recognize this character. The Introvert is a type that is well known to everyone.

But are all those people who get energy from downtime anti-social in the way Jung describes? In my experience, I have seen many individuals who are introverted – in that they restore themselves through alone time – but who are neither anti-social, nor sagacious, nor interested in personal growth. The quiet surfer who likes parties just fine comes to mind as one example.

Likewise for Jung, Extravert is sometimes equated with drawing personal identity from the tribe. 'Extraverts, and all people who are identified with their personas, fear to be alone because they begin to see themselves.'[72] Does he really mean all outgoing people are averse to self-inquiry? Certainly a segment fit this description, but the question should be: Does every Extravert fit it? Is it possible that further differentiation of the meaning of Introvert and Extravert is required?

While Toni Wolff probably helped Jung to construct his model of *Psychological Types*, she had a lingering feeling that it was missing something. In 1934, she outlined a way of describing some of the qualities that we see bound together in Introversion and Extraversion separately. We'll look at it in Chapter 6.

SENSATION AND INTUITION

In Jungian typology, Sensation and Intuition are functions by which we gather information. Sensation is the apprehension of reality in all of its outer tangible forms; Intuition is the apprehension of reality in its holistic form. Where Sensors see the trees, Intuitives see the forest.

Sensation happens through the conscious awareness of the senses. Sensors are hands-on gifted appreciators of the world's colours, textures, tones and tastes. They are the best at remembering (and sometimes recreating) detail-rich impressions of the world. If you have a friend who can hear a song once and then play it, they're a Sensor. They are good at being present in the moment and aware of their surroundings. You want your hairdresser, portrait painter and your brain surgeon to be a Sensor.

Intuition happens through the unconscious. The Intuitive rocks the whole; they just get it, even without knowing why. Intuitives are natural-born pattern finders. They uncover associations, connections and meanings quickly and often. Intuitive types apprehend hidden inner tensions and future possibilities – they see where the trend is going. They get how all the pieces fit together. Intuitives can be good at picking up what people are trying to communicate underneath their words; they understand body language, subtle messages and other interpersonal cues. This can make them better at relationships.

The Greek philosopher Plato, with his attention to wholes and to the operating principles of nature, epitomizes the Intuitive's point of view. Aristotle, with his use of all of his senses and close attention to every detail, epitomizes the Sensate way.

The gift for melody is a uniquely Sensor form of genius. Brian Wilson and Paul McCartney illustrated their genius through the songs they wrote for the Beach Boys and The Beatles. Another form of Sensate genius is artistic mastery of performance, the virtuoso who delights in creating through playing with notes, tone, volume, rhythm and attack on the instrument. Masters such as Jimi Hendrix, Jerry Garcia and Jackson Pollock exemplify the Sensor genius fluidity, with complexity of form on the fly in the moment.

And yet where there is genius, there is often an overemphasis of attention on one part of life. Sometimes those Sensors who are

Plato (left) is a classic example of the Intuitive, while Aristotle (right) is an example of the Sensate.

so attentive to the details of reality will miss what the Intuitive sees via body language. Sometimes even master Sensors have trouble in relationships or other areas of life in which the Intuitive is gifted – and vice versa.

Where the genius Sensor creates through fluidity with intricate detail, the creative Intuitive has a sense for the whole. The Intuitive is ahead of the game, as a business leader with an original concept or a nose for where the market is going. The Intuitive knows how best to put all the pieces together. The singer-songwriter Peter Gabriel (the original lead singer of Genesis) describes himself this way, saying that he's not particularly gifted at any one part of his music, but has a gift for bringing the whole production together. But being drawn to the holistic has the drawback of risking missing the concrete: 'The intuitive is a type that doesn't see, doesn't see the stumbling blocks before his feet, but he smells a rat for ten miles.'[73]

In the world of dating and mating, the division between Intuitive types and Sensate types may be the hardest to overcome. This is because they simply perceive experience in opposite ways: Sensors see the plethora of fine detail that fills our experience of the outer world; Intuitives read between the lines and see the hidden possibilities. If they go to a party, the Sensor will see the beautiful green taffeta dress, remember the little bit of cinnamon in the smell of the warm apple pie, and notice the newly painted wall. Meanwhile, the Intuitive will get a feeling that two friends are having sex on the sly, get a great idea for a new business idea, and notice the tense body language between a couple. In the song 'She's Your Lover Now', Bob Dylan has a line that sums up the vast gulf in communication expectations that can exist between a concrete-type Sensor (him in this case) and the Intuitive partner: 'Now you stand there expectin' me to remember something you forgot to say.'

THINKING AND FEELING

The third category of personality type is Thinking and Feeling, and it describes our innate approach to decision-making. Thinkers tend to judge objectively, meaning that what is fair is for everyone to be treated alike. Feelers tend to judge subjectively, meaning that what is fair is for each person to be viewed on their own merit and within their own real context. Thinkers may feel more comfortable with logical approaches; Feelers with personal approaches.

Thinking tells us what something is; Feeling tells us how we feel about it. Feeling comes from the unconscious; it's hard to change the way we feel about something. Thinking is a conscious process. Thinkers tend to want to understand and then respond in a rational step-by-step way. They are drawn to logical principles and systems which organize the world around us.

When a person is living a Feeling-directed life, we think of them as being empathetic and accommodating, softer and more people-oriented. When a person is living a Thinking-directed

Bob Dylan neatly highlights the division between the Intuitive and the Sensate types in his song 'She's Your Lover Now'.

life, we think of them as being questioning, more systematic and perhaps colder and impersonal, less people-oriented.

Typology proposes that everyone has a dominant function which provides most of their energy. For Introverts, their dominant function is directed inwards; for Extraverts, it is directed outwards. Jung's own dominant function was Introverted Thinking – naturally reflecting on the objects that he saw in the world and categorizing them, and thinking about them logically. Introverted Thinkers seek to understand the world around them through an inner process of reflection.

By contrast, Extraverted Feeling types express their emotions, judgements and attitudes with others regularly and openly. They enjoy social engagements and business networks, and may feel drawn to large organizations. Their life emphasizes attendance to their own and to others' Feeling values and to warm interpersonal relationships.

An Introverted Feeling type lives a life full of emotion that may be mostly unexpressed. They may also have a strong sense of right and wrong; whether they express it is another matter.

An Extraverted Thinking life is full of rules and principles; they like to categorize the world and tell you why. They understand why an engine works and want to tell you all about it. They work things through rationally.

DEVELOPMENT AND MATURITY

Where everyone has a dominant, superior function that provides most of their energy, there follows a second-most preferred function that also gets a lot; a third, or tertiary, function which gets less still; and finally an inferior function. The inferior function is our least adept function, and often suggests an area of life that we may neglect.

Our dominant function is the way of life that comes easiest for us – what we are best at doing. A dominant Sensor might be a master of flavours, or sounds, or touches. A dominant Sensing type has their energy going towards picking up all of the concrete

An Extraverted (left) and an Introverted man.

world around them. They craft with intricate precision; they know the catalogue and can recite the canon chapter and verse. Their inferior function is its opposite, Intuition. They may have less fluidity with that and miss subtle relationship clues, for example. We have the virtues of our vices, as the Greeks say.

However, Jung observed a special way in which the unconscious flows into our inferior function. This is our least reliable function, but sometimes the magic in our creative process happens there. A Sensing creative may be able to construct a beautifully worded poem, but not know what the poem's meaning is until it's done. Their capacity for detail allows them to create splendid forms, but since Intuition is their inferior, they may not know the point of the poem until the unconscious works it in, to their great surprise. In the reverse type, an Intuitive creative will know the meaning of the story before they begin, but the right way to say it will come only through the unconscious. Their inferior function being Sensation means that the magic happens in their process of word-crafting, and can't be willed into form reliably.

Over the course of a lifetime, we increase our fluidity with our tertiary and inferior functions and integrate them further but not completely. Our primary mode of functioning most often remains dominant across our lifespan, although we may find more and more of our interest goes into the less preferred functions.

Typology points to possibilities of shadow and neurosis. Being gifted in one part of life and relying upon it for success often means that there are other parts of life we don't even see. To some extent, our personality type is the water we breathe, it's the essential nature of our way of being. Our inferior function often suggests potential shadow qualities that we may have, challenges to our character or qualities we need to work on developing further.

Jung observed that the neurotic often over-relies on their dominant two functions and avoids needing to use the latter two. '. . . the endless conflicts of neurotic natures, nearly always rest on a noticeable one-sidedness of the conscious attitude, which gives absolute precedence to one or two functions, while the others are unjustly thrust into the background."[74] Here, he's pointing out a direction in which we can look for imbalance within ourselves: how much do we move through the world predominantly according to our dominant function? Which of these functions do we use least or are the least fluid for us? If we look, we might see part of our shadow there.

Personality type can help us to recognize our gifts and get a better handle on our weaknesses. It can help us appreciate the strengths that others are bringing to the table and the challenges they may be going through.

Differences in type are one of the reasons why relationships are necessary for growth: people of other types lead us into seeing things about ourselves that we miss, and help us to explore new ways of perceiving, being and valuing.

Key Points

- *Psychological Types* – in this book, published in 1921, Jung introduced the terms *Extravert* and *Introvert* (and others) into common usage.

- **Extraversion** – in common usage, an Extravert is someone who is outgoing and talkative. Jung's Extraversion is an attitude of interest in the outer world. The Extravert gets energy through interactions with people, their energy moving out to meet the objects of the world. The Extravert is likely to be calmed by stimulation.

- **Introversion** – in common usage, an Introvert is someone who is shy, socially reserved or awkward. Jung's Introversion is an attitude of interest in the inner world. The Introvert gets energy through solitary time, and their energy reflects on the world's objects. They may be overwhelmed by too much stimulation.

- **Sensation** – the function of collection of information through the senses. Sensors perceive reality in keen detail and are able to retain a great amount of sensory data. Sensors have an appreciation for the tangible, and may miss inferences and subtle meanings.

- **Intuition** – the function of collection of information through the unconscious. Intuitives perceive holistically and have a good sense for the big picture. They may have a nose for what is unspoken or hidden or for what may be emergent, but they may miss concrete details.

- **Thinking** – a preference for an objective decision-making style. Thinkers often operate with a detached, logical and consistent value system. They question thinking and appreciate principles. They are sometimes thought of as tougher or colder than Feeling-type people.

CHAPTER 6
Archetypes

WHAT IS AN ARCHETYPE?

We all understand the power of instinct. We recognize in ourselves, our children and others the expression of biological forces. Instincts are particular patterns that nature drives us to express physiologically. They are universal through the human species; we see them in action all across the world. They also extend throughout nature; animals share many of their instincts with us. Instincts are blunt forces: they move us from deep inside, and we don't know why but we can't resist their pressure. They drive us – and they drive all beings to have, for example, built-in fears, whether of predators, snakes, dark caves or heights. Instincts shape our responses to the world well before we're aware of such programming within us.

The 19th-century German philosopher Arthur Schopenhauer's idea of prototypes inspired Jung's conception of archetypes.

Instincts express themselves through patterns living within us biologically, and Jung saw similar forms acting within us psychologically. Continuing in the tradition of Plato, Kant and Schopenhauer, Jung took an ancient Greek word for first principles – *archetype* – and used it to refer to the universal patterns he was discovering in the psyche. An archetype is an 'inherited mode of functioning, corresponding to the inborn way in which the chick emerges from the egg, the bird builds its nest, a certain kind of wasp stings the motor ganglion of the caterpillar, and eels find their way to the Bermudas. In other words, it is a "pattern of behaviour."'

In Jungian psychology, the term *archetype* is used to describe powerful forces within the unconscious that lead us to 'build our nest the way we do'. These deep psychological structures form the foundation of our attitude towards life and our way of dealing with the world. Given a certain stimulus, how do we react? Why do we react one way and someone else reacts oppositely? Why do some people approach problems head-on while others pause to reflect? Archetypes inform not only what we do, but how we apprehend the world – what it is that we see out there. Our inner affiliation with certain archetypes creates our unconscious view of the world and goes a long way to defining our character. Archetypes influence our fascination with particular ideas and inform how we feel about certain people. Behind our psychological projections – the values we unconsciously invest into others – lies our relationship to archetypes. In a similar way to complexes (and one can have an archetypal complex), archetypes can have us more than we have them, and we may not know it. If something 'makes your skin crawl', there may be an archetypal response at work, operating unconsciously.

Perhaps the best metaphors for archetypes are our ancient mythological gods. The Greek pantheon provides us with: Ares, God of War, who symbolizes the aggressive instincts; Hera, Goddess of Marriage, the maternal instincts; and Dionysus, God of Wine, our pull towards revelry, altered states and orgiastic

A statue of the Greek God of War, Ares, who presents an archetype of the aggressive instinct.

pleasure. The stories associated with each figure illustrate a central principle, a direction of their energy, an attitude towards life, but also a correlated shadow, a path through which their downfall or difficulties come into being. Each god is a holistic character, usually with a good and bad side, as well as a uniformity of approach to the world which enables us to imagine what they might do in almost any situation.

All around the world at one point in time, our ancestors worshipped their own figures similar to these. What is it about mythological gods like these that moves us to see ourselves in them? Why did each particular Greek citizen go to that particular temple? Why did they choose their god? Jung believed that archetypes were numinous centres of tremendous energy and even awe and wonder in us, and thus they inform our values and our spirituality. Our inner affiliations with archetypes suggest the principles that carry the most importance for us and bring with them a whole package of related potential psychological positions. Our relationship to a host of these energies inside us helps to define our character to a great extent. We identify with the mythological gods because they represent the deepest energies inside us.

Archetypes are collective patterns, found universally throughout human cultures. It is common today to think that we have outgrown our ancestors' fascination with such figures, but their pull on us remains. We see them in what is popular. The bestselling novels of Neil Gaiman place literal archetypal figures right at the centre of the action. *American Gods* (2001) is built around a character called Shadow, and has been adapted successfully for television. Today, films based on characters from comics, sometimes starring mythological figures, are the biggest box office draws. However, in some ways these films are myths retold without meaning – without the power to transform the audience psychologically. Our ancient ancestors used storytelling and drama to evoke a change in those watching. Contemporary stories are, for the most part, made to sell and to entertain.

In this chapter, we'll explore the archetypal level of the psyche – what Jung called the *collective unconscious*. We'll briefly look at a few examples, including the Hero and the Wise One.

THE COLLECTIVE UNCONSCIOUS

Jung first started using the term *archetype* in 1919, but his conception of it was preceded by a dream from 1909. In his dream, beautifully described to Bennett and others, he starts in his house in a room with a study much like his, but discovers a door down to the ground floor. Taking the stairs, he enters a room filled with furniture from the sixteenth century or earlier. Proceeding to the cellar, he finds it is all of Roman design. And then:

> *I got an uncanny feeling going down the staircase with a lantern in my hand. I thought now I am at the bottom. But then in a corner I saw a square stone with a ring in it; this I lifted and looked down into a lower cellar, which was like a cave or possibly a tomb. Some light came in as I lifted the stone. The cellar was filled with prehistoric pottery, bones and skulls. I was quite amazed . . .* [75]

Jung spent a good deal of time reflecting on this dream and its 'atmosphere of expectancy'. Eventually, it dawned on him that the dream represented the layers of the unconscious, beginning with the personal – he starts in his house – and descending to levels that were no longer his own, but shared. He told the dream to Freud, who sought a personal explanation for it at the time, but would later talk about 'archaic heritage' and 'memory traces', praising Jung for his pioneering work on this view. The dream depicts what Jung calls the *collective unconscious*.

Jung proposed that in addition to personal consciousness, there exists a deeper stratum in the psyche which is universal, impersonal and shared by all individuals. It is not developed by our personal experience, but inherited. We see it in the activity of pre-existent forms that shape our experience of the world – *archetypes* – which we gain sight of only through their effects

Jung's dream of a country house, which had layers built at different times in parallel with the different layers of our own unconscious, inspired his idea of the archetype.

on us psychologically. Our discovery of the activity of these contents comes only through inner reflection; most of the time, the archetypes operate through us unconsciously. The collective unconscious is the presence of the past living through us.

> *The collective unconscious comprises in itself the psychic life of our ancestors right back to the earliest beginnings. It is the matrix of all conscious psychic occurrences, and hence it exerts an influence that compromises the freedom of consciousness in the highest degree, since it is continually striving to lead all conscious processes back into the old paths.*[76]

Here, Jung is pointing out not only the existence of the collective unconscious, but also its danger. He is saying that the well-worn pathways of previous generations are alive and well within us, and calling us to return to them. Our personal freedom and our ability to make conscious choices is impeded by the collective unconscious; it's shaping our view of the world and of

147

ourselves. One way we can see this notion echoed today biolog-ically is in the discovery that trauma is carried epigenetically through families – the past is forming us and our present. The collective unconscious is the psychological force bending history to repeat itself.

But why does history have any form at all?

Plato saw the existence of meaningful forms in the world as evidence of a purposiveness in life. Archetypes were an expression of an ordering principle which structured the universe into forms. Likewise, for Jung, archetypes were not just an operative collective memory, but an expression of the root metaphors of all of the world's mythology living within us.

Jung was seeing in clients' dreams strange images which also appeared in ancient alchemical texts that he knew they could never have seen (an observation only possible in his era, a time before the arrival of television and the Internet). This echoed the recurring motifs he found in literature and mythology, which also suggested to him an inherited rather than a culturally transmitted shared psychological structure within us. Archetypes are symbolic wholes – they include a range of meaningfully related images and possibilities, and both negative and positive expressions. 'Such variable representations cannot be inherited. The archetype *is a tendency to form such representations* of a motif – representations that can vary a great deal in detail without losing their basic pattern.'[77]

We may ask, as well, that if there is a form-making quality to nature, doesn't that suggest an intelligent spirit at work in the building blocks of our reality? We'll explore more of the 'Big Questions' in Chapter 8.

In New Age spirituality, the collective unconscious is used to refer to the psyche as a singular unitary field, which was not Jung's intended meaning. The great Jungian analyst and author Marie-Louise von Franz observed that 'it is naturally very tempting to identify the hypothesis of the collective unconscious historically and regressively with the ancient idea of an all-extensive world-soul."[78] However, Jung did have many experiences of shared psychic events across time and distance, and he did not believe the psyche was limited to the physical body. For him, the big question was whether or not the figures of the inner life, such as those of the archetypal world, were in some sense real on their own. He believed that they were, and spoke of the collective unconscious as the objective psyche, a living reality that is not bound to any particular person, but existing nonetheless.

THE ARCHETYPAL HERO

Creation stories aside, there is perhaps no theme more common in mythology than the myth of the Hero. The Hero is the strong one who faces the monster and overcomes it, representing one of the most basic energies of life. Fight or flight? The Hero fights. He stands his ground. He confronts the beast and survives. He makes the kill. This is the basic instinct to assert ourselves in the world, and is one the most fundamental facets of existence. Aggression and power; that dynamic within us which rises to face the world, and which is the character of the archetypal Hero.

The Hero is the protagonist in the story. He is the eternal doer. From the most primitive cave paintings to Homer's tale of Odysseus, humanity knows the story of the Hero. Joseph Campbell has described the story of the Hero as a universal mono-myth, a story omnipresent in human mythology. His famous work *The Hero with A Thousand Faces* (1949) describes the Hero who goes to the underworld, survives his torments and returns with a bounty for the tribe. That pattern is repeated throughout our early stories.

Campbell was influenced by Jung in his observations about the archetypal Hero. In turn, Campbell's work inspired George Lucas in his creation of *Star Wars*. The Hero's quest places Luke Skywalker in conflict with a technological monster that must be destroyed. Luke succeeds for the benefit of the whole galaxy. In these stories, the Hero is seen within the context of positive relation to the tribe, but we can also examine the Hero on his own.

The literature professor Joseph Campbell demonstrated that the core motifs of the Hero's journey are repeated in almost every story.

To look at the doer of heroic deeds beyond the social context is to see the archetypal Warrior.

The archetypal Warrior is the energy of competition for competition's sake, the drive to see who is the best – running to see who is the fastest, for example. The archetypal Warrior within each of us is our ambition, our willpower, our strength; it is how comfortable we are asserting ourselves. The Warrior is expressed in society by those who get their identity through doing, through prowess, through success and achievement. A Warrior is someone whose sense of self can only be injured on the battlefield, the sportsfield or at the finish line. Being the best matters here.

Toni Wolff described this type of character among women in her 1934 lecture on *Structural Forms of the Feminine Psyche.* Her

Amazon form is a Warrior: she derives her sense of self from her capacity for action, her strength and her self-sufficiency. She does not get her identity from anyone outside herself. Today, we see this way of being lived out by men as much as women in worlds such as business, sports and the arts. The singer-songwriter Grace Jones expressed this dynamic well: 'I like conflicts. I love competition. I like discovering things for myself. It's a childlike characteristic, actually. But that gives you a certain amount of power, and people are intimidated by that.'

The Warrior archetype is neutral, neither good nor bad, but also brings a shadow that many avoid seeing. Its shadow is

The strength and self-sufficiency of the Amazon form provides the archetype of the Warrior.

aggressiveness, violence, anger, meanness or cold distance. The Warrior's shadow is the 'strong man', the brute who takes what he wants because he can, because he's the strongest. In the 1980s, David Mamet's play *Glengarry Glen Ross* (1984) and Oliver Stone's *Wall Street* (1987) showed us the Warrior energy as profit-seeking without concern for personal or social costs. This energy is one of the prime drivers of our civilization.

There is even a drive within us to conflate physical dominance and moral goodness. For hundreds of years, someone's virtue or the rightness of their claim could be determined through battle; a duel could decide who was correct in the 'eyes of God'. There is the belief amongst those predominantly moved by this archetype that winners win and losers lose – and so be it. The Warrior archetype is a philosophy of life for many.

The archetypal Hero is the defender of the tribe, the Warrior is an impersonal archetype. It is common today to speak of the Hero archetype without including the Warrior and his shadow. We have sanitized the archetypal Hero. In many modern archetypal systems, some, including the Jungian analayst Robert L. Moore, consider the Warrior mostly in the context of their relation to society, and in that way miss much of the archetype's natural shadow. In the New Age movement, the term *spiritual warrior* gets used in a similar fashion, and seems to have more in common with the Wise One or Shaman archetype than with the lived energy of the Warrior.

In mythology, the gods of war are often shown with their shadow included. We see their downfall through aggressiveness or through acting without thinking. We are shown the character in full, and those identified with the archetype are invited to see what might save them personally in the end. In our culture today, the spaces of the Warrior archetype are often those in which thoughtful reflection is avoided or even mocked. The Warrior fuels the rip-on-your-mates language of the locker room and the construction site. It thrives in the boardroom and the country club; it celebrates the dominance of power over all else. In this way, the archetypal Warrior is insulated from the uncomfortable sight of what it might be missing; it avoids being confronted with its shadow.

THE KING OR QUEEN ARCHETYPE

The King or Queen is the alpha, the leader or dominant person in a tribe or group. One cannot conceive of the King or Queen without the collective that surrounds them; the ruler and the tribe are a single psychological organism. Our relationship to this archetype in us is expressed through the way we feel about society and authority. It connects very strongly to how we view the established power in a community or nation, how we feel about authority figures, and often how we feel about the status quo.

Those who personally identify with the King or Queen archetype find solace in social order. The structure and stability of the group comforts them and makes them feel safe and secure. They are oriented towards the values of the collective to which they belong, and they take care of their own. They tend to be team players, and their team are the good guys. They are invested in what their community has achieved. They tend to

The King archetype seeks stability and order, and takes comfort from the social group to which he belongs.

fear change and hate chaos. They endeavour to bring and defend structure and order.

The King and Queen know who they are and what they want. There is often a strong executive function in those who identify with this archetype; they're comfortable making decisions. As a result, many such folk (though not all) have a preference for the Judging function of the Myers-Briggs Type Indicator™.

In their book *About Men and Women* (derived from the work of Toni Wolff), Noreen and Tad Guzie talk about the Father and Mother archetypes as the everyday inflection of the King and Queen. The Guzies see this archetype in individuals who get primary satisfaction out of *doing for* others, and who find identity and fulfillment in the group, the family, the tribe or the company. The Mother and Father understand themselves through their place in the tribe, and often choose service-oriented careers such as teaching, firefighting, nursing or law enforcement. They can make excellent leaders because their unconscious is invested in the group. At their best, Mother and Father provide the healthy structure and order that creates generativity (the promotion of industriousness, usually in subordinates) in their children, their employees or their communities. They have an instinctive gift for blessing, for making people feel like a part of a special team and letting us know that we're included.

Because these folk derive so much of their identity from the group, issues of interpersonal respect, saving face and 'keeping up with the Joneses' are often at the forefront of their awareness. They don't want to be made to look bad publicly. However, the core of the shadow of Mother/Father tends to surround issues of control, power and hierarchy. Those who identify with the King or Queen often demand respect for their authority, as expressed by the phrase 'My way or the highway'. When Richard Nixon told David Frost in 1977 that 'when a President does it, that means that it is not illegal', he was expressing his personal identification with the King archetype; he was the law.

Since the 1950s, Western society has increasingly dethroned

Richard Nixon exemplified the King archetype, as he demanded that his authority was respected.

men who are Father archetypes. It used to be the case that the alpha-type Father male was the wheel around which society revolved. The evolution of men's groups and the men's rights movement is in large part a response to this shift. Today, men who identify with the Father archetype are searching for new ways to understand themselves. Jordan Peterson, the Canadian psychologist and professor, approaches Jung by emphasizing the Father-King approach, and his popularity comes in part through speaking to those experiencing the difficulties of this societal change and to young men looking for Father archetype energy in the world.

One can also have a Father complex, a personal neurosis vis-à-vis one's Father. Such a condition can have positive or negative forms, and nearly everyone has some kind of parental complex. One classic form of the Father complex is the Senex-type personality. *Senex* refers to the Old King who is constricting the life around him to protect his power. He is the authority whose unconsciousness and insistence on stability blocks the natural flow of growth. The Old King must be defeated in order for the process of life to advance. He fears the chaos that the new brings. In mythology, Chronos, the God of Time, eats his children to protect his reign, a kind of conservancy that kills new life in us. We can experience the Father complex as a negative scolding voice inside ourselves, as an inner refusal to grow, or as life lived unconsciously expressing some of these aspects in actions and attitudes towards others.

Just as we can carry this archetype's negative qualities out into the world, we can also perform its best aspects. Robert L. Moore beautifully expressed the archetypal King (or Queen) in their fullness as someone who can see your gold shining and not hate you for it. The mature Father- or Mother-type person does not envy you for your gifts, but cherishes them as they cherish you. Blessing others is a special gift for those close to this archetype. A mature Father- or Mother-type person is gifted at making those around them feel seen and appreciated.

Those who identify personally with the King or Queen archetype can sometimes associate it with Jung's concept of the Self. Robert L. Moore and others do this explicitly; Moore's map of the psyche places the King or Queen at the top. Jung himself

An engraving of Chronos, the God of Time, who would eat his children to keep his throne.

never made this assertion and, in fact, he connected the Self with the archetypal Child as much as or more than the King or Queen.

THE WISE ONE

The Wise Old Man or Woman is a figure found throughout folklore and mythology. They possess superior understanding and also often a more developed spiritual or moral character. Frequently, such characters provide the information or learning that the Hero needs to move forward in their quest. In *Star Wars*, Ben Kenobi plays the teacher to Luke, introducing purpose and knowledge into the young Hero's life. Where the Hero brings drive, courage and direct action, the Wise One introduces the importance of the opposing values of thought and questioning. Jung describes it thus: 'Often the old man in fairytales asks questions like who? Why? Whence? Whither? For the purpose of inducing self-reflection and mobilizing the moral forces.'[79]

The Wise One may appear in disguise to test the character of others. In the second *Star Wars* film, *The Empire Strikes Back* (1980), Luke's mentor Yoda does not reveal himself as such when they first meet. He waits, asking questions that test Luke's motivation for being there. Jung associated the Trickster archetype with the Wise One, and the use of disguise emphasizes this correlation.

The Sage fits under this general archetypal category as well. The Guzies' definition of this more particular archetype defines it as the figure who uses rational, conscious awareness and knowledge to achieve goals. This character type is value-neutral and not necessarily good or bad, nor even wise. The Sage finds identify and fulfilment through their intellectual power. 'Sage's "inner drive is to put himself and others in touch with reason, mind, thought, spirit . . . His best contact with others takes place through the sharing of ideas and theories and visions . . . . . . Found not only in the professions of teaching and scholarship – he might be a cabinet maker, a mechanic or a gardener, a 'cracker-barrel philosopher.'"

The Wise Old Man archetype often tests the character of other archetypes while helping their development.

Toni Wolff observed that in contrast to the Sage, there is also a character type which generates knowledge through the unconscious. She called this structural form of the psyche the Mediatrix or medial woman, the one whose inner awareness brings access to information through non-rational means. Wolff herself was this type, as was Jung's mother and grandfather. Jung himself lived in both Sage and Mediatrix forms. 'The nature that my mother possessed on her other side was the voice of nature that uttered deep truths, shattering truths.'[80]

Examples of this archetype in history include the Oracle of Delphi, Nostradamus and others. There is also the unfortunate historic period in which women who possessed this kind of awareness were dubbed witches and burned at the stake for it.

Our culture's urge to deny the existence of non-rational knowing was relieved by projecting their shadow onto these victims.

The Wise Woman or Crone is also often connected to this kind of knowing, and Jung explicitly described the Shaman as 'the one who mediates the unconscious'.

THE ARCHETYPAL CHILD

Our mythological and religious systems are also full of the tension between parent and child. Part of what defines us psychologically is the conflict between father and son — consider, for example, *Star Wars*' Luke Skywalker and Darth Vader. But what is it that gives the Child enough power to hold his end of the fight? What is it that he brings to challenge the established power of his Father? The archetypal Child brings the new.

Just as reality has principles that hold everything together, it also has principles that invite the next evolution into being. The Child archetype represents the strongest, the most ineluctable urge in every being, namely the urge to realize itself.[81] For Jung, it was the archetypal Child, not the archetypal King, who represented the most powerful urge in us, the drive to individuate.

As described earlier, Jung discovered that the child was still alive inside him and possessed 'the creative life which he lacked'. The Child archetype represents nature's capacity to endlessly produce unique new life, and the never-ending capacity for becoming in each of us. Jung also said famously that the new comes from playing with objects that we love. In this way, we can associate the Child and Lover archetypes.

Toni Wolff described a structural form of personality which is constituted by the archetypal Child and the archetypal Lover, called the *Hetaira* or Companion. She is the muse who meets the other one-on-one, and whose attention helps them to grow. The Guzies' form of this archetype is called the Seeker – the brother-sister type, the one who relates non-hierarchically, the one who plays and is called to become more of themselves. The Guzies noted that these archetypes represent fully realized ways of being, and are not a stage towards living out another archetype. It's possible to live a mature life that is in touch with archetypal Child.

Jungian psychology also describes a related Child complex. The Puer or Puella (Latin for *boy* or *girl*) is a figure who remains forever young. As a complex, the Puer or Puella describes the condition of immaturity, an inner refusal to grow up. This person typically remains attached to the mother well into adulthood and may expect the parent to be there to back them, financially or otherwise.

Marie-Louise von Franz in her book *The Problem of the Puer Aeternus* looked at these issues through *The Little Prince* by Antoine de Saint-Exupéry. Her remedy for the Puer's dilemma was for him to come down to Earth and come into form in the world. The classic Jungian answer to his complex is to do one's

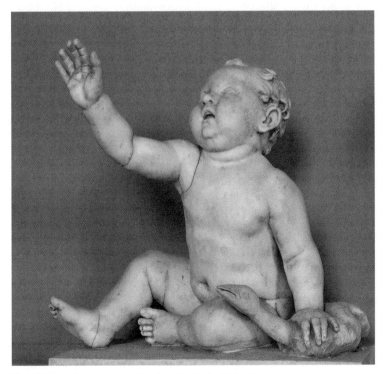

The Child archetype embodies the drive to individuate.

own work, whatever that may be – to complete something of value for the world.

Jung emphasized that simply cutting off the energy of the child, as many people do en route to adulthood, creates the conditions for bitterness and dissatisfaction in midlife. Instead of this, Jung invites us to rediscover the playful child inside of each of us. We can make a choice to live with the energy of the archetypal Child. Jung calls us to connect with 'the boy who is born from the maturity of the adult man, and not the unconscious child we would like to remain.'[82]

TENSIONS IN THE TRIBE

Jung begins his exploration of personality type with a single division. On one side he sees the Extraverted Feeler, and on the other, his own point of view, the Introverted Thinker. His book *Psychological Types* was an attempt at breaking apart these two types. In her lecture on *Structural Forms of the Feminine Psyche*, Toni Wolff added what she thought was missing from this system. Others have continued to try to improve the ways in which we delineate and categorize these differences in personality, and this field remains a work in progress.

Wolff saw her work as an addition to *Psychological Types* rather than a correction, but looking at it today, we see that her structural forms make it possible to break apart Jung's overgeneralized Extravert and Introvert Types more accurately. Jung's Introverted character is a combination of getting energized from the inner world or downtime, reflective understanding (sagaciousness) and an inherent orientation towards personal growth. Jung's Extravert is a combination of getting energized from social interaction, an approach that moves directly towards the objects of the outer world and an orientation towards society and collective values. Those broadly defined associations are proven insufficient as soon as we meet a quiet surfer whose energy moves to meet the objects of the world head-on, or a reserved person who is neither sagacious nor identifies with collective values.

Wolff's structural forms and the Guzies' archetypal system allow us to clarify each those categories separately: the energy of meeting the world head-on is the attitude of the Warrior and Amazon; reflectivity is the way of the Sage and Mediatrix; and identifying with collective values is the position of the Mother and Father archetype (King and Queen). Using such a definition allows us to retain the common understanding of Extravert and Introvert as being related to being energized by social interaction or by downtime.

However, Jung was correct in identifying the general polarities in the psyche. He recognized a core division in the unconscious. There is no single universal map of growth for all people, but rather there are polarities which define us and make us who we are. There are profound differences in the way people see the world, and directly opposing ways of valuing. Jung's description of the archetypes enables us to better wrestle with these eternal questions. These kind of polar insights into human nature aid us in understanding ourselves and those around us. But they also ask us to look at uncomfortable qualities that may lie at the base of our cultural divisions.

As the unconscious speaks in symbols, the collective unconscious speaks in the language of our shared symbols. What metaphorical buttons have juice for us, what makes us stand up and salute? Which of the ancient mythological figures might be alive in us today?

Key Points

- **The Collective Unconscious** – Jung postulated that beneath our personal unconscious lies a deeper shared stratum of the psyche. Its unity of inner architecture contributes to the preponderance of shared mythological forms across cultures. It is our shared inheritance of collective memory and the home for seemingly timeless psychological forms: archetypes.

- **What is An Archetype?** – the nerve centres of the Collective Unconscious. They are symbolic wholes – they have a multiplicity of image forms that are meaningfully related. Our relationship to particular archetypes may provide the foundation of our attitude towards life and of our way of dealing with the world.

- **The Hero Archetype** – the one who acts in the service of his tribe. The Hero is the eternal defender and protector at the centre of our dramatic tales. This timeless figure is the protagonist of a great preponderance of our mythological and religious stories.

- **The Archetypal King and Queen** – these symbolize the principles of order, generativity and blessing. Wolff and Moore related these archetypes to the archetypal Mother and Father. Father's status has changed in Western culture over the last century.

- **The Wise One** – the figure of superior knowledge or morality. Often older, this character leads the Hero to a required learning or something essential. It symbolizes our capacity for reflection and understanding. Figures of the Wise One include the Trickster, the Crone and the Shaman.

- **The Archetypal Child** – symbolizes the world's endless capacity for the new. The archetypal Child is expressed in us through our unending capacity to become more whole, to individuate, to become who we are meant to be.

CHAPTER 7
Anima and Animus

WHAT ARE THE ANIMA AND ANIMUS?

Every man carries within him the eternal image of woman, not the image of this or that particular woman, but a definite feminine image. This image is fundamentally unconscious, an hereditary factor of primordial origin engraved in the living organic system of the man, an imprint or 'archetype' of all the ancestral experiences of the female, a deposit, as it were, of all the impressions ever made by woman – in short, an inherited system of psychic adaptation.[83]

With those words, Jung powerfully described of the nature of the archetype of the eternal woman in us, what he called the *Anima*, one of the most powerful forces in the psyche. Likewise, what he called the *Animus* is the archetype of the eternal male. This archetype is both personal and archetypal – a bridge figure between the ego and the collective unconscious. In our personal experience, this inner figure tends to be of opposite character to our ego or persona, and to hold opposing values. The character of this figure also often consists of the opposite personality type that dominates consciousness. If we are a Thinking type, the inner figure will be a Feeling one. Most commonly in our experience, this figure is projected outwards – onto the person with whom we fall in love at first sight, for example. Our inner figure can be the object of our heart's desire. But Jung observed far more going on there: this figure played a role in bridging the personal and collective unconscious in our inner life, and was often the source both of tremendous suffering and of great potential growth.

While traditionally Jungians have spoken of the Anima or Animus as our sole contrasexual opposite, today the Jungian clinical and scholarly world hosts a variety of ways of looking at how best to describe the appearance of these figures in different individuals. Beebe, for example, suggests that we may have a ratio of Anima to Animus of 3:1, or vice versa.

Jung saw that people's outer character often had a contrasting inner quality, an unconscious 'other' that held complementary but

A photograph of Carl Jung in 1922. In the early 1920s, he developed ideas of the Anima and Animus.

rejected ways of being. While the persona is our ego's consciously held values and most comfortable approaches, our Anima (from the Latin for *soul*) or Animus (from the Latin for *mind*) is (often) an inner contrasexual opposite that expresses the inner opposite set of values and approaches with which we are uncomfortable, and which we have the least fluidity in applying.

> *It pleases you, however, to play at manliness, because it travels on a well-worn track. . . . But humankind is masculine and feminine, not just man or woman.*

> *You can hardly say of your soul what sex it is. But if you pay close attention, you will see that the most masculine man has a feminine soul, and the most feminine woman has a masculine soul. The more manly you are, the more remote from you is what woman really is, since the feminine in yourself is alien and contemptuous.*[84]

As our character is forming, certain values are emphasized and some are left undeveloped. There is a tendency in the human psyche for some people to have at the foremost of their awareness Logos: clarity, distinction, objective truth. Likewise, there are some people who have Eros: relatedness or feeling is dominant in their attention and way of being. In the most general sense, the Masculine-oriented ego has within him a whole world of Feminine values that are in the background of his consciousness, so to speak. But nonetheless, they are present.

As a consequence of being a Thinking-type personality, Jung found that he had been rejecting the Feeling-type values inside himself, and that his inner Anima figure bore a Feeling character. He also personally felt that he had an inferior relationship to relatedness. This realization led him to working on that part of his life. The drive towards individuation leads us to come into contact with those less conscious qualities in ourselves, especially in the second half of life. Jung discovered this quality in himself through the presence of his own negative moods, which were full of affect but of suspect character. How do we relate to an opposite set of values? How do we deal with vulnerability, intimacy, relatedness?

To the extent that the Anima or Animus operate unconsciously, they are likely to be experienced in negative forms. Without conscious relationship, the Anima expresses itself as moodiness and can even come to consume us in a negative attitude about life. The Animus expresses itself as 'inferior judgements, or better, opinions'[85] that exercise a powerful influence on our emotional lives and on our attitudes towards life and the world. Ann Belford Ulanov noted that the Animus can take the form of 'emotional expectations of how things ought to be done or understood, expectations which are compulsively expressed and devoid of sense of timing.'[86] The Animus can lead us to doubt ourselves and our own ideas, and towards dogmatism and an overly critical attitude towards ourselves and others.

Both Anima and Animus are autonomous complexes that pressure the ego. We experience the Anima most often as a singular figure, and the Animus as a group of male figures. Ann and Barry Ulanov explored a fully fleshed-out view of the Anima and Animus in *Transforming Sexuality* (1994), showing their life-giving quality and setting them on an equal footing. Dr Edward Santana examined the relationship of these figures to sexuality in *Jung and Sex* (2016).

When we are children, the Mother or Father may hold for us the Anima or Animus image. As we grow, we first experience it when we fall in love. Often, especially with love at first sight, we project our Anima or Animus onto the person we love. When the Anima is projected, we are in adoration. Because of this archetype's timeless quality, the person with whom we fall in love may seem to remain the same age and always seem 'just as beautiful as the day we met'. Anima fascination is frequently expressed in art and, for example, in songs such as 'Every Little Thing She Does Is Magic' by the Police or Eric Clapton's 'Layla' and George Harrison's 'Something' (apparently written for the same woman, Pattie Boyd). Here, we see the Anima as obsession, and very much beyond our control.

The powerful compulsion of these inner figures points to their potential for creative transformation and healing. The same energy that drives us into compulsive obsession can fuel us to creative heights and deep personal growth. This process is shown famously in the life of Dante Alighieri, author of *The Divine Comedy*. At the age of nine, Dante met Beatrice and was immediately captivated: 'Behold, a deity stronger than I; who coming, shall rule over me.' Marie-Louise von Franz noted that Beatrice is the figure who eventually leads Dante up to Paradise, but this happens only after he has spent a long time in Hell. Before the Anima figure leads him into contact with the timeless figures of the unconscious, it first puts him 'into a hot cauldron where he is nicely roasted for a while.'[87]

While the contents of the Anima and Animus (images, thoughts, affects) are personal, the archetype itself and its role as mediator to the collective unconscious are not personal. These inner figures direct us towards a greater relationship to the unconscious and the Self, but they can do so only if we relate to them consciously. That conscious relationship is the transforming act, but it usually does not happen without discomfort or neurosis.

Katz noted the similar function of Dakini figures in some forms of Buddhism. He recounted the story of Nāropā, a spiritual teacher in medieval India who received such a strong encounter with an inner female figure that he resigned his post and abandoned all worldly honours. Nāropā had a powerful vision of an old, ugly woman who 'mercilessly revealed to him his psychological state.'[88] Previously, he had lived a life of the mind, of the analytical Masculine principle, and had missed entirely the world of feeling and emotion. She represented all that he had failed to develop in himself and showed him a half of life that he was missing entirely. Here, the Anima used a negative image to force a necessary constructive realization that ultimately connected him to the real force of the Self within him.

The medieval Italian poet Dante Alighieri was driven by the compulsion of his Anima.

Nāropā was an 11th-century Buddhist from India. His story highlights how the Anima can lead to self-realization.

While the modern mind tends to dissociate and not relate to the inner contents consciously, doing so allows for deep transformation and for the superior insight of these figures to be received. That achievement requires making them as conscious as possible, dialoguing with them (using active imagination) and recognizing and accepting their messages for us. The pull of these inner figures eventually resituates consciousness between the ego and collective unconscious, allowing for greater relativity of awareness. The figures can ultimately lead us to a healthier attitude towards life, as the archetypes of life. The contents of these figures can be integrated, but the Anima or Animus itself cannot be. Jung saw it as a lifelong task to remain watchful for the presence of this inner guide in our life, most often by paying attention to our moods and opinions.

THE FEMININE AND THE MASCULINE

In Jungian psychology, the terms *Feminine* and *Masculine* are used to refer to archetypal forms of energy present in the psyche. These terms are drawn from the wisdom traditions of ancient and medieval cultures, both Western and Eastern. The ancient Chinese observed the reality of the Yin and the Yang at play in the world. The alchemists spoke of the principles of Eros (feeling) and Logos (truth), and the notions of Solar and Lunar principles. It is from those conceptions that Jungian approaches to the Feminine and Masculine are drawn.

For modern readers, it is important to understand what Jungians are *not* saying in using these terms. They do not describe how anyone should be or behave, nor prescribe gender roles. In describing the archetypal Masculine, Jungians are not talking about men, and in describing the archetypal Feminine, Jungians are not talking about women. Both qualities are present in everyone. While Jung observed that men typically have a Feminine inner opposite (the Anima) and women a Masculine inner opposite (the Animus), each person is an individual and will be a new and unique expression of these traits. There are many

Yin and Yang, two opposing forces at work in the world, are described as the 'Feminine' and 'Masculine' in Jungian psychology.

women who are predominantly Masculine in their psychology, and there are many men who are predominantly Feminine in theirs. The Jungian approach to the Feminine and Masculine describes the flow and expression of both of these qualities in all people. It is also used to explore unconscious cultural imbalances that are pertinent to the crises of our time.

The archetypal Masculine is associated with the bright, drying light of Solar daytime and doing, activity, objectivity, rationality, certainty, distance from what is observed, abstraction, ego consciousness and an 'upward' spirituality. The great Israeli Jungian analyst and author Erich Neumann observed that the acts upon which consciousness and the ego are built up are objectifying actions that separate the observer from the observed. The 'scientific method is a typical example of this process: a natural connection is broken down and something is isolated and analyzed, for the motto of consciousness is *determinatio est negatio.*'[89] Jungian analyst Jeffrey Raff describes the Masculine as the knight with the sword, which symbolizes the 'world of conscious thought and discrimination, and the ego's ability to categorize, label, evaluate and discriminate. The cutting edge of the sword is the mind's sharpness, which separates experiences into their individual parts so that understanding may be gained.'[90]

The Masculine is that part of our consciousness which understands the world through separation from it and objective distance. Many of the world's cultures tend to place more value on this approach than on the modalities of its opposite.

The archetypal Feminine is associated with the moist, fecund darkness of the soil and night-time, and with being (allowing natural processes to run their course), non-action, context, subjective relatedness, feeling connection to others (Eros), the unconscious, matter, the body, the earth, the miracle of life, nature and immanent or 'downward' spirituality. The archetypal Feminine is associated with the sustaining matrix of life and the unity of the Mother and Child. According to Freud:

'Mother' is an archetype and refers to the place of origin, to nature, to that which passively creates, hence to substance and matter, to materiality, the womb, the vegetative functions. It also means the unconscious, our natural and instinctive life, the physiological realm, the body in which we dwell or are contained; for the 'mother' is also the matrix, the hollow form, the vessel that carries and nourishes, and thus it stands for the foundation of consciousness.[91]

One of the primary myths of the archetypal Feminine is the Demeter-Persephone story which came to underly the Eleusinian Mysteries. Demeter is the Greek Goddess of life and vegetation, of fields and plants and all of the green growing things. Persephone, her daughter, is abducted by Hades, the God of the Underworld. At the story's end, Persephone is resolved to live for a third of the year in the Underworld, but to emerge again each spring to be with her Mother. Thus, the cycle of life is symbolically recognized, understood and honoured. A magic is pointed to that lives in the world outside of ourselves. Baring and Cashford described this as follows: 'As a nature myth, Persephone is the seed that splits off from the body of the ripened grain, the mother, when sinking beneath the earth, she returns in the spring as the new shoot. The etymology of her name "she who shines in the dark" suggests that the seed does not actually die but continues to live in the underworld, even though it cannot be seen above.'[92]

An ancient Greek vase depicts the mythological story of Demeter and Persephone.

The archetypal Feminine is also associated with the highest forms of embodied spiritual insight as personified in figures such as Guanyin (the Goddess of Compassion), the Virgin Mary, Mary Magdalene and the biblical co-creatrix figure of Sophia, or Wisdom, as described in Proverbs 8:26–31: 'When he fixed the heavens firm, I was there, when he drew a circle on the surface of the deep, When he thickened the clouds above, when the sources of the deep began to swell, When he assigned the sea its boundaries – and the waters will not encroach the shore – when he traced the foundations of the earth, I was beside the master craftsman at play everywhere on his earth, delighting to be with the children of men.'

Guanyin, a bodhisattva known as the Goddess of Compassion, exemplifies the Feminine archetype.

In contrast to Masculine understanding through separation and distance, Feminine awareness is process-oriented and relational, according to Jungian analyst Ann Belford Ulanov: 'The Feminine mode gives us the wiles to live next to the gap, from which new symbols or refurbished old ones emerge. But when they come they are strange to us, full of ambiguity, with uneven edges, a crude power, an unsettling spirit. It is the feminine way to hover over this gap.'[93] The Feminine is that part of our consciousness that understands the world through connection to it and related empathy. Many of the world's cultures devalue this way of being.

For Jungians, the Masculine and Feminine are archetypal – timeless forces that operate within us predominantly unconsciously. We use the words as frames for describing libido or psychic energy in the hopes of better understanding how they are moving through as individuals and as a collective. They are metaphors we employ to try to gain insight into the powers inside us.

Both have intrinsic strengths and shadows, both have regressed and mature forms, both have areas of life that they are exceptionally gifted at understanding, and parts of reality that they miss completely. Of course, neither principle is believed to be better than the other, and a healthy integration of both (at least symbolically) is likely to be a measure of health. Certainly, an imbalance in favour of one or the other could contribute to psychological illness.

Jung and others see historic periods as having characteristics of one or the other. Jung saw one of the primary cultural diseases of our time as a value system that privileges Masculine values over Feminine ones – and recognized that this system would be called into question:

> It is said that always when one principle reaches the height
> of its power, the counter-principle is stirring within it like a
> germ. This is another, particularly graphic formulation of the

psychological law of compensation by an inner opposite . . .
Whenever a civilization reaches its highest point, sooner or later
a period of decay sets in. But the apparently meaningless and
hopeless collapse into a disorder without aim or purpose, which fills
the onlooker with disgust and despair, nevertheless contains within
its darkness the germ of a new light.[94]

THE FALL OF THE MASCULINE IDOLS

Jung believed that we need to understand ourselves within the cultural story of our time. Accurately naming the psychological narrative that drives us, including its dominant unconscious voices, is necessary in order to save ourselves.

Looking around him, Jung saw that the old stories no longer animated most people. As Nietzsche and Fitzgerald both said: 'God is dead' in our time. Spirit had left the churches and migrated; the Gods were in flux; the psychologically dominant principles inside of us were changing. A period was ending and a new one beginning.

A wide tradition of Jungians and others sees the Masculine and Feminine lenses as useful frames through which to unfold our psychological history, the journey of our evolution of consciousness. These stories share a beginning in a paradisiacal unity of our early creation stories, a splitting off of the Masculine and a neglect of the Feminine, and a yearning for reunion that characterizes our time. This frame sees the emergence into scientific modernity as having been driven by a pursuit of objective clarity, which increased the distance created by rationality and cut off our connection to body, earth, feeling. Today, our time is characterized by an imbalance in favour of Masculine approaches, yet that impetus seems to have reached its peak.

Where there had been a Masculine dominant zeitgeist behind our history's development, today we seem to be seeing that principle's end. Our time is defined by ever-deeper revelations of evidence of the dark side of Masculine institutions: the #MeToo movement, the cover-up of abusive priests within the Catholic

Church, the financial crisis. Ours is the time of the fall of the Masculine idols: modern sports is a parade of former heroes become villains, from drug and sex scandals to murder. But how did we get here? And how does Jung's lens help us see the problem more clearly?

The earliest figures of human reverence celebrated nature and the miracle of life. Objects of worship such as the Venus of Willendorf, depicting a full-bodied female form, reflect our early ancestors' wonder at life itself. 'The earliest human intuition of the sacred was that the earth was the source of all life and ground of being.'[95] One sees the Feminine here as reflecting a deep mystery, as Jungian analysts Anne Baring and Jules Cashford describe: 'The mystery of the female body is the mystery of birth, which is also the mystery of the unmanifest becoming manifest in the whole world of nature. This far transcends the female body and woman as carrier of the image, for the body of the female of any species leads through the mystery of birth to the mystery of life itself.'[96]

The initial phase of human religious worship was one that celebrated our place within the natural world. Our earliest ancestors walked in a world that they saw as full of meaning, seeing signs and symbols throughout their experience. But as Lévy-Bruhl has noted, this kind of enmeshment with the world is an undifferentiated awareness – what he called a *participation mystique*. Jung saw this state as a unity within the unconscious, with no conscious discrimination between fantasy and true meaningful symbol.

In this initial state, all possibilities are hosted equally and no differentiation is made. This initial phase is dominated by the Feminine, and as Esther Harding describes, Mother Nature is both good and bad: 'she tolerates all things . . . for nature consists necessarily in growth and decay.'[97] This is one of the qualities that makes the Feminine different from the Masculine, a serving of the process of nature without expectation. As celebrated Jungian author and analyst Marion Woodman has written, the Feminine

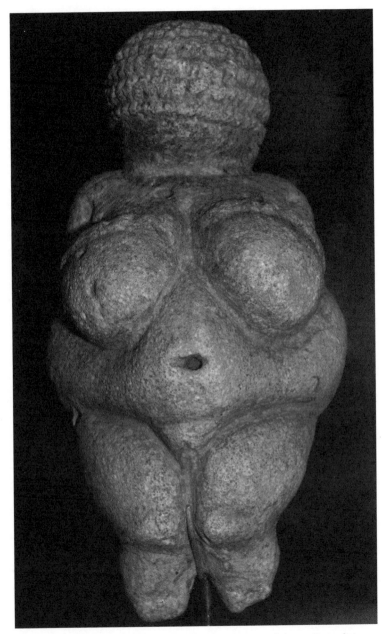

The Venus of Willendorf, made c.30,000 BCE, was one of the earliest religious objects ever made.

'gives us the courage to love an acorn without knowing what an oak tree is.'[98] That quality of reception is increasingly lost as the Masculine develops.

As is described in stories such as the expulsion of Adam and Eve from the Garden of Eden, for example, the Masculine emerges with the clarity of rules ('Thou Shalt') and immediately begins to repress our body, the earthly, the sexual and the Feminine. Quickly, the notion of sin is associated with women. And while morality requires the repression of instinct, the objectivity that the Masculine employs divorced it from the awe for the miracle of life and left it alone in the universe: 'The Western mind has been founded on the repression of the feminine – on the repression of undifferentiated unitary consciousness, of the participation mystique with nature: a progressive denial of the *anima mundi*, of the soul of the world, of the community of being, of the all-pervading, of mystery and ambiguity, of imagination, emotion, instinct, body, nature, woman – of all that which the masculine has projectively identified as "other".'[99]

Increasingly since the Scientific Revolution, our energy has been redirected out of wonder for nature and into fascination with our own creative capacities. We've become enchanted with our ability to conquer the world. Having so much information about the world, we've come to confuse measurement for mastery, and fallen into an inflated state of awe at ourselves. Our technology has given us the capacity to say: 'Let there be light' and with the flick of a switch, it's there. If we look closely, we'll see that psychologically many people today place the reverence that we previously had for something divine into our technological gadgets. Today, we look for God in our mobile phones.

We see this in our fantasies for the future. Science fiction shows us worlds that are hyper-technological, often featuring cold, sterile decor. In other words, we psychologically believe that we'll continue to move further away from nature. We express this through seeing the universe as a clockwork (a human invention) and nature as a machine. When we see nature as a machine, we can see ourselves as only biological robots. Then we can also see computers as having the same consciousness as humanity (artificial intelligence). Each of these are metaphors for our unconscious grandiosity.

Jung greatly feared our inflated unconscious investment in our own science and technology. He described ours as a time of Kairos: 'the right moment — for a "metamorphosis of the gods", of the fundamental principles and symbols. This peculiarity of our time, which is certainly not of our conscious choosing, is the expression of the unconscious man within us who is changing. Coming generations will have to take account of this momentous transformation if humanity is not to destroy itself through the might of its own technology and science.'[100] Writing after World War I, Jung described our collective state in a way that includes the reality of humanity's shadow and a warning about us being the danger to ourselves:

We are also the disappointment of the hopes and expectations of the ages. Think of nearly two thousand years of Christian ideas followed, instead of by the return of the Messiah and the heavenly millennium, by the World War among Christian nations and its barbed-wire and poison gas. . . . [We have] seen how beneficent are science, technology and organization, but also how catastrophic they can be.[101]

Jung believed that it was our Masculine imbalance leading us into the crisis of our time, and our own belief in reason, technology and science and a lack of appreciation for the Feminine and the unconscious which threatens us with destruction. We see a tremendous drive in Masculine ideologies to split spirit from body and hasten our arrival 'up there' through a final confrontation.

We see the loss of the Feminine in cultural diseases such as materialism. Rather than consciously celebrating nature, the earth and the miracle of life, we unconsciously, compulsively seek it through materialism: possessions. That connection has become

A painting of the first Thanksgiving at Plymouth, Massachusetts, in 1621. Today, the sales that follow on 'Black Friday' overshadow the holiday itself.

explicit in the United States, where the Thanksgiving holiday is now overshadowed by the following day's 'Black Friday' orgy of consumerism. Esther Harding said: 'Something is amiss in the Western male psyche: Not only has he lost the feminine, but he is not interested – he doesn't even know that he has lost it.'[102]

With all of our psychic energy moving into abstraction, our connection to the life of nature and instinct has lessened. Neumann noted that in the pursuit of better behaviour and moral action, we've cut ourselves off from instinct. But it's gone too far. Today, we know that we're in our heads too much. It's not hard to see that something has been lost by placing so much of our attention into devices. Our overstimulated culture is a bird that feels like it has nowhere to land. Many people feel like, or operate as though, they've lost feeling for life.

Perhaps the most direct way we can see the operation of the unconscious Masculine inflation within us is through the lack of concern in our culture for the destruction of the planet. Only a society that is split off from nature inside itself, from the Feminine, could strangle the life out of its Mother, the planet on which it lives. While we've imagined ourselves to be moving forward into fantasies of the future which are further away from nature, climate change draws us back into it and forces us to see the reality of our existence in a finite world. We are being brought back down to earth to face the shadow of what we have done.

Yet some believe that even within our time of crisis, there are signs of hope and even of purpose. The archetypal historian Richard Tarnas observed that the long process of the historic separation of the Masculine from the Feminine seems to point towards the inevitability of a coming reunion. Beneath the alienation and other symptoms of our era, there ultimately lies a drive to recover our connection to the whole, to rediscover the Feminine and soul in the world, to appreciate wholly our existence within the mystery of life, to come home and find ourselves a place again within the universe. 'For the deepest passion of the Western mind has been to reunite with the ground of its being.'[103]

A statue of Gaia, the female personification of the earth. As society has increasingly cut itself off from the Feminine, this has led to damaging the planet itself.

Jung saw reasons for hope in the increasing connection to the Feminine in our culture. He considered that the adoption by the Catholic Church of the Assumption of Mary as dogma – a change made in 1950 as a response to popular pressure (and not papal insight) – symbolized a step towards the reintroduction of the missing element.

We might also see the Feminine as being reintegrated in our time through cultural trends such as the rise of femininism and pro-ecological values, respect for indigenous peoples, tolerance for a variety of perspectives, the urge to reconnect with the body and emotions (as expressed, for example, by an increasing interest in yoga and healthy eating), and an interest in the unconscious and the inner life. The instinct to reconnect with these qualities echoes the Feminine zeitgeist and is ever-increasing. There is an urgency within us to reconnect with what has been neglected inside of us. Marie-Louise von Franz said: 'Now the archetype of the feminine, the archetype of the goddess, has become constellated in the collective unconscious. That's why all these different movements flare up all over the place. They all call for a recognition of matter, of nature of the irrational, of eros, of sexuality, of the importance of the physical. And this is also connected with the individuality of women, and her values with the values of eros, with the feeling relationship.'[104]

In our time, not only must the Masculine light of truth be used to face its shadow and see the harm it has caused; it must also open itself to consider mysteries it is imagined do not exist. Jung's work did this in ways that few others have matched. While the whole project of leading us to see the reality of the unconscious is his greatest service to the repressed Feminine, perhaps most emblematic of the conscious integration of the Feminine and Masculine principles is Jung's work on synchronicity.

Synchronicity is the phenomenon of the momentary meaningful correlation of outer events with inner states. Jung coined the term to refer to occurrences that showed symbolic purpose present within the field of the individual and the world.

The Assumption of the Virgin Mary *by Peter Paul Rubens, c.1616–18.*

Often synchronistic occurrences happen in situations charged with emotion, with affect, with feeling. Perhaps you run into a past lover travelling on the same path you had previously travelled together; and then you realize that you had taken that same trip with each other ten years before, to the day. Synchronicities often reflect powerful emotional realities inside us and suggest that we live a world that seems built for them to happen, that values them and brings them into being. Appreciating them opens us to a wider worldview, one in which reality is full of meaning and that somehow spirit really is in matter. Such a form of understanding can be described as an archetypal Feminine one – and we'll look at it in much greater detail in the next chapter.

For further reading on this topic, please see the work of Marion Woodman, Ann Ulanov, Baring & Cashford, Andrew Harvey and Sufi Llewellyn Vaughan-Lee, *The Fires of Desire: Erotic Energies and the Spiritual Quest* by Halligan and Shea, the author's own *Crop Circles, Jung and the Reemergence of the Archetypal Feminine*, as well as the epilogue to Richard Tarnas's *Passion of the Western Mind* (available online).

Key Points

- **Anima and Animus** – our inner contrasexual figure or figures that express values opposite to the persona or conscious personality. This inner figure is often projected onto an external other, but can be related to intrapersonally and act as the bridge to the collective unconscious.

- **Feminine and Masculine** – two modes of being that operate in all people, regardless of gender. The Feminine is associated with yin or lunar qualities of receptivity, being, Eros (relatedness through feeling), matter, feeling, the earth and nature's processes, including the miracle of life. The Masculine is associated with yang or solar values, including direct action, clarity, certainty and Logos (truth).

- **Fall of the Masculine** – one of the ways that some Jungians and others view our current era is as the end of a period of predominantly Masculine values and the beginning of a period in which the Feminine and Masculine are in greater balance.

CHAPTER 8
Synchronicity

ON ALCHEMY

Alchemy is an ancient branch of natural philosophy, the study of nature which led to modern science. Alchemists used chemical procedures to try to transmute base metals into more valuable ones, gold in particular. But the various formulae in alchemists' writings can also be seen as symbolic metaphors for the transmutation of the personality. The *lapis philosophorum* (philosopher's stone), which was the goal of their work, can be seen to represent the drive for self-realization.

Alchemy was practised across the world, including Europe, Africa and Asia. It originated in Graeco-Roman Egypt in the first few centuries AD, and the term *alchemy* comes from the Arabic word *al-k miy* , in turn based on the Greek *kh meia*, meaning the art of transmuting metals – and from which comes the English term *chemistry*. It is both a scientific and spiritual tradition that continued in large part through

Carl Jung was fascinated by alchemy, and he sought to apply alchemical insights to psychology.

A page from a 15th-century alchemical manuscript. Jung collected a series of manuscripts like these.

beautifully illustrated manuscripts full of arcane symbols and procedural drawings.

Jung was an avid collector of medieval alchemical manuscripts. In the final third of his life, he dedicated a great deal of time to studying them alongside Marie-Louise von Franz, who translated many of them for him. The manuscripts depicted stages such as the *mortificatio* and the *nigredo* (blackening), dark nights of the soul when the ego

confronts the shadow. They showed him an alchemical wedding: the alchemist and his counterpart, *soror mystica*, enter into a bath (*coniunctio*) and are subjected to heat, purified and transformed. They are brought together into a new, higher order unity, the *hieros gamos* – the sacred marriage. Images of sexuality, including those of the androgyne and hermaphrodite, are seen as having symbolic psychological meaning and pointing to forms and qualities of inner transition and movement.

Alchemists saw metals as having emotional characters: 'Silver is touchy, iron is brave, copper sensuous.' Each can be seen as having a quality or two it can share with us: 'honesty, cruelty, passion.' Here, metal has become equivalent to an archetype inside of us. 'Alchemical symbolism is particularly useful for illustrating the consciousness transformation that results from our interaction with the numinous.' In this way, rather than containing chemical formulae, alchemy is seen to contain spiritual wisdom. It offers descriptions of the way we grow, the nature of its operations reflecting the suffering of life by which we are transformed into who we are. Alchemists included an appreciation of their own feeling states in their operations, just as Jungians include their own feelings in the process of analysis.

Where depression can be seen alchemically as a symptom of too much lead, in Jung's psychology symptoms are understood to express *inner* imbalances – too much or not enough of something inside of us. But such suffering can be looked into, and we can gain insight into the activity of the unconscious through reflective practice and inner listening. As Jungian analyst and

author Monika Wikman writes, 'cultivating a living relationship to the mysteries of the psyche depends on our ability to gain into the darkness, dim the light of ego and attend to what appears.'[105] Thus, we can build a relationship with these inner figures and try to hear what they are expressing otherwise as symptoms. In this way, alchemy offers a pathway to a deeper appreciation of the meaning behind psychological symptoms, and helps us to understand what is being spoken in our suffering and fantasies.

The 1475 manuscript Pretiossimum Donum Dei *shows the three processes of* nigredo *(blackness),* albedo *(whiteness) and* rubedo *(redness).*

Alchemists valued deep interpersonal intimacy and observation, and Jung's psychology reflects this in his description of the transference-countertransference field – the shared psychic space experienced between analyst and analysand. His essay 'On The Psychology of the Transference' uses the alchemical wedding stages to illustrate the nature of psychotherapeutic relations. But perhaps the greatest insight that Jung drew from alchemy was a patience for the natural process of the psyche. He saw the ways of the inner world as having their own forms and the ego as existing within a living psychological ecosystem: the unconscious. 'Only after I had familiarized myself with alchemy did I realize that the unconscious is a process, and that the psyche is transformed or developed by the relationship of the ego to the contents of the unconscious.'

As the individuation process progresses, the ego becomes less aligned with the personal consciousness and moves closer to the contents of the collective unconscious (a notion shared with Buddhist psychology). Over time, we develop a personal connection to the timeless inside of us. Jung recognized the need that we have for this content not just as an idea, but as a felt reality. The stages of alchemy describe the difference well. In an interview with mythologist Mircea Eliade, Jung described the alchemical *albedo* or whitening stage as producing a consciousness that is ideal but too divorced from real life. 'In order to make it come alive and have "blood", it must have what alchemists call the *rubedo*, the "redness" of life. Only the total experience of being can transform this ideal state of the albedo into a fully human mode of existence.'[106]

Alchemy is an hermetic art, an outlaw spirituality. Samuels, Shorter and Plaut noted that Jungian and Freudian psychologies were both, in their time, seen just as alchemy was in its time, 'as a subversive and underground force: its vivid and earthy imagery contrasting with the stylized and sexless expression of mediaeval Christianity, just as psychoanalysis startled Victorian prudishness and complacency.'[107]

Jung published *Psychology and Alchemy* in 1945, and *Mysterium Coniunctionis* was published shortly after his death, in 1963. For further exploration of this topic, and in addition to Jung's writing on the topic, see Marie-Louise von Franz's various works on alchemy; Jeffrey Raff's *Jung and the Alchemical*

Imagination and *Wedding of Sophia: The Divine Feminine in Psychoidal Alchemy*; Thom Cavalli's *Alchemical Psychology*; and Monika Wikman's *Pregnant Darkness: Alchemy and the Rebirth of Consciousness.*

SYNCHRONICITY

In 1930, Jung coined the term *synchronicity* to describe incidents in which outer events come together in a way that clearly reflects inner states. Commonly spoken of as coincidences, Jung had observed these strange effects for many decades and had begun speaking about them with Albert Einstein nearly 20 years before. He also had the good fortune to be able to discuss them with the Nobel laureate physicist Wolfgang Pauli (who was both an analysand and friend). Einstein had shown that time and space were relative to each other, and in synchronicity Jung saw the relativity of matter and psyche. Synchronistic phenomena make evident the fact that spirit and matter are not divided from one another, but instead are a part of a larger whole whose existence is revealed only in such moments. Jung described this greater unity as the *Unus Mundus*, or one world, in *Mysterium Coniunctionis*.

One classic example is that of a patient who was telling Jung her dream of a golden scarab. At just that moment, he heard a tap at the window. After a second tap, he went to the window to open it up – to find a flying scarab beetle, which flew inside and into his hands. Jung opened them before the patient, saying: 'Here is your scarab.' The incident broke through the patient's over-rational attitude and helped her to have a transcendent experience that connected her meaningfully to something deeper inside. As Dr Cynthia Cavalli explained: 'The recognition that an inner event is inexplicably connected with an outer event stuns the individual out of a normal worldview, giving them a glimpse of the larger patterns at work in life, and in turn radically altering their attitude, which allows acceptance and healing.'[108]

Sometimes the synchronicity doesn't bring about the healing, but reflects it. Jungian analyst and author Ann Belford Ulanov

One of Jung's patients recounted a dream involving a scarab beetle, which proved to be the catalyst for a breakthrough.

provides a clinical example. A male client struggled to describe his painful childhood experience of being locked in a dark attic as a punishment for crying too much. Eventually he reached a moment of personal revelation, and recognized the connection between this trauma and a compulsive, fascinating fetish he had. At the moment in which he reached this new attitude, the attic in his childhood home was struck by lightning. Only the attic was destroyed.[109]

In his autobiography, Jung tells the story of being excited to ask Freud about precognition and parapsychology on a trip to Vienna in 1909. While Freud was keen on researching those fields at the end of his life, he was sceptical at this time and shut down Jung's whole inquiry. Jung describes their disagreement:

While Freud was going on this way, I had a curious sensation.
It was as if my diaphragm were made of iron and were becoming
red-hot – a glowing vault. And at that moment there was such a
loud report in the bookcase, which stood right next to us, that we
both started up in alarm, fearing the thing was going to topple over
on us. I said to Freud: 'There, that is an example of a so-called
catalytic exteriorization phenomenon.' 'Oh come,' he exclaimed.
'That is sheer bosh.' 'It is not,' I replied. 'You are mistaken, Herr
Professor. And to prove my point I now predict that in a moment
there will be another such loud report!' Sure enough, no sooner had
I said the words than the same detonation went off in the bookcase,
to this day I do not know what gave me this certainty. But I knew
beyond all doubt that the report would come again. Freud only
stared aghast at me.[110]

Jung's story shows us the presence of emotion – Jung's, if not
Freud's too – and the apparent displacement of that energy into a
nearby bookcase. Jung felt it in his body before it happened. Is such
a phenomenon even possible? Michael Shermer, the publisher of
Skeptic magazine, was so struck by a similar experience that he
published it in *Scientific American*.[111] Jennifer, his fiancée from
Germany, had shipped her belongings over to his home in Beverly
Hills, CA. Among them was an heirloom electronic radio that
had belonged to her grandfather, who had been her only father
figure but passed away when she was only 16. They tried to fix the
radio, but to no avail. On the day of their wedding, she was feeling
that something was amiss and wishing that her grandfather could
be there to give her away. She took her soon-to-be husband to a
back bedroom to speak alone. In the room they could hear music
playing, but couldn't figure out from where.

We searched for laptops and iPhones . . . At that moment Jennifer
shot me a look I haven't seen since the supernatural thriller
The Exorcist *startled audiences. 'That can't be what I think it is,*
can it?' she said. She opened the desk drawer and pulled out her

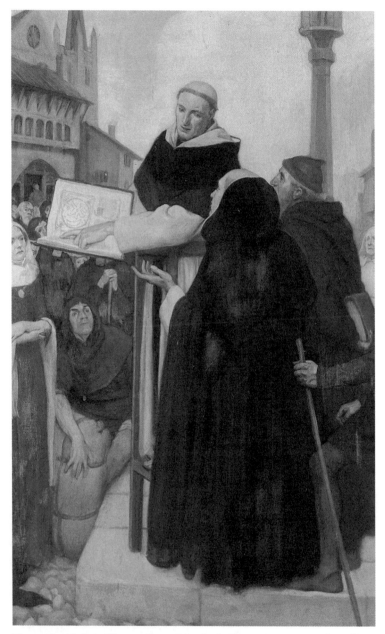

The medieval cleric Albertus Magnus taught St Thomas Aquinas, and was later canonized himself.

grandfather's transistor radio, out of which a romantic love song wafted. We sat in stunned silence for minutes. 'My grandfather is here with us,' Jennifer said, tearfully. 'I'm not alone.' Fittingly, it stopped working the next day and has remained silent ever since. . . The eerie conjunction of these deeply evocative events gave her the distinct feeling that her grandfather was there and that the music was his gift of approval. I have to admit, it rocked me back on my heels and shook my skepticism to its core.'[112]

In all of these examples, matter comes together to clearly reflect or express someone's inner psychological state. Matter is animate momentarily. There is powerful meaning present in each of these examples, and they either cause or echo a genuine personal transformation. Synchronicities can change our attitude about life, our *Weltanschauung*, and one of the elements that we are most likely to miss in these events is the presence of feeling. Jung saw that emotionality, in particular, played a special part in generating the field that led to the coordination of outer events with inner meanings. 'Synchronistic phenomena occur for the most part in emotional situations; for instance, in cases of death, sickness, accident and so on . . . We observe them relatively frequently at moments of heightened emotional activation, which need not however be conscious.'[113]

Human cultures have been observing the interactivity of feeling states and events for thousands of years. The alchemists spoke of their vision of this unitary reality as the *Unus Mundus*, while in ancient China this concept lived in the philosophy of Taoism. For the Taoists, our inner feeling reality is what carries us through the chaos of life successfully. Authenticity, sincerity and humility are the actions by which we find the right path. To believe in the Tao is to believe that the world is navigated through feeling. Here, the reality of the shared field of inner state and outer world is assumed as a given. A notion of a sympathy between all things in the world was also a part of Hermetic thought and other European traditions since medieval times. In 1250, Albertus

Magnus, a teacher of St Thomas Aquinas, wrote: 'A certain power to alter things indwells in the human soul and subordinates the other things to her, particularly when she is swept into great excesses of love or hate or the like . . . For a long time I did not believe it...[but] I found that the emotionality of the human soul is the chief cause of all these things.'

For us, accustomed as we are to privileging thinking and rationality, it is a radical notion to imagine that feeling could play such a 'magical' role in our reality. For Jung, synchronicity reveals the world to be both purpose- and meaning-filled. It necessitates the adoption of a far deeper, more complex and more loving view of reality than one offered up by Western rationalism. Synchronicity reveals the mechanistic worldview to be, at best, a preliminary stage to be outgrown but, at worst, also perhaps a psychological illness.

Jung considered the over-rational attitude of our time, one facet of which is called *scientism*, to be the symptom of a Masculine imbalance and a sickness in our culture. We privilege

A Taoist master from a 16th-century Chinese painting. In Taoist philosophy, following one's inner life provided the guide to navigating the real world.

rationality and certainty and deride vulnerability, intimacy and a sense of connection to others and the world. The scholar Richard Tarnas described the importance of synchronicity to the crisis of our time. The phenomenon has a 'special relevance for the schism in the modern worldview between the meaning-seeking human subject and the meaning-voided objective world.'[114]

While we've imagined ourselves to be the only subject in the universe, synchronicity shows us a reality in which subject and object are always interwoven. Meaning is always available to us. Shamanistic and divinatory practices tap into that field in order to heal. 'The principle of synchronicity brings the long-lost unity of the world again within the reach of modern thinking, and acts as a compensating element in the disunion and dichotomies of our time.'[115] Even Michael Shermer, a chief of the sceptical world, was moved enough by his own experience (described above) to say that 'we should not shut the doors of perception when they may be opened to us to marvel in the mysterious.'[116] Discovering that we live in such a reality affords us both a privilege and a responsibility. The author J. Gary Sparks said: 'The spirit and matter issue is something we are all being called to face. The task of our time is to make life in time and space, the relationship to physical events in life, the sacred altar of being.'[117]

Truly understanding that we live in a world in which synchronicity happens, and recognizing that events can be brought together to bring healing and greater consciousness, asks something of us. We are asked to put ourselves into life more fully, to live it out, to meet that astounding fact with the whole of our being. And not only understanding these events with our thinking minds, but also allowing the truth and power to hit us emotionally is what brings us to experience meaning and affords us healing. Marie-Louise von Franz said: 'The realization of "meaning" is not a simple acquisition of information or of knowledge but rather a living experience that touches the heart just as it touches the mind.'[118]

A further challenge for us is to avoid interpreting synchronistic events only in a personally aggrandizing way. It is commonly thought that a synchronicity is only a blessing, missing larger possibilities that may be afoot. 'For synchronicities have a shadow side, as in the exaggeration of the trivial to discover a self-inflating meaning.'[119] Today, we're used to being consumers and expect to have our synchronicities mean what we want them to mean. But they only point to the involvement of 'the Gods', the archetypes that might be at play, not which ones. So we should look not only for what we want to see, but for what wants to be seen by us.

It should be remembered that synchronicities often seem to compensate for imbalances in the psyche, just as the unconscious does through symptoms and dreams. Jung tried to live this understanding as best he could, even when it meant seeing something he didn't want to see about himself. Henry Fierz described an encounter with Jung, illustrating what that looked like.[120] In the 1950s, Fierz was hired to prepare for publication a book that had been written by a scientist who had recently died. Before going ahead with the project, the publishers wanted Jung's opinion of it. They met at 5 pm, and Jung announced to him that he did not think that the work should be published. Fierz disagreed, and their discussion grew 'sharp':

> *Jung looked at his wristwatch, obviously thinking that he had spent enough time on the matter and that he could send me home. Looking at his watch he said: 'When did you come?'*
> *I: 'At five, as agreed.'*
> *Jung: 'But that's strange. My watch came back from the watchmaker this morning after a complete revision, and now I have 5:05. But you must have been here much longer. What time do you have?'*
> *I: 'It's 5:35.'*
> *Whereon Jung said: 'So you have the right time, and I the wrong one. Let us discuss the thing again.'*

In perhaps the perfect Swiss synchronicity, Jung allowed his newly repaired malfunctioning wristwatch to show him 'what time it was'. He allowed himself to recognize that there was something that he wasn't understanding about what was happening. He gave himself enough play with the symbolic quality of reality to allow into his awareness the thought that he might be the one who was 'off' here. Rather than privilege his ego above the unconscious, Jung looked at these events for what he might be missing. J. Gary Sparks explained: 'It is addressing life in the present that cleanses and heals a festering wound. Jung never tired of saying this. After the past is explored, additional inquiry into yesterday does not lead to further healing. A change of attitude into the present does, and this change of attitude is exactly the business of a synchronicity.'[121]

Jung finally published his first essay 'On Synchronicity' in 1952. Further recommended reading includes: *On Divination and Synchronicity* by Marie-Louise von Franz, and *C.G. Jung's Psychology of Religion and Synchronicity* by Robert Aziz. Finally, for a truly grand historical journey, see *Cosmos and Psyche* by Richard Tarnas.

Although he repaired his watch, Jung was willing to concede that there may be something more to the reality of time than what it told him.

Carl Jung wrote a book entitled Answer to Job *in 1951, which sought to apply his psychoanalytic methods to the biblical character of Job.*

ANSWER TO JOB

During a febrile illness in 1951, Jung wrote a 100-page essay that became one of the most profound and controversial books of the twentieth century. *Answer to Job* looks at a biblical character whose life God allows to be destroyed over a bet with the Devil. It examines the role that humanity plays vis-à-vis God in the Bible. It puts the Judeo-Christian God image on the couch – which gives the book its power and infamy. Jung wrote *Answer to Job* in a week, but it was the summation of forty years of thought. 'The book has always been on my mind,' he told Mircea Eliade in 1952.

Having been the son of an unfulfilled clergyman and a spiritualist mother (and grandfather), having had a numinous dream of a phallic God-image as a young boy, and having pursued the spiritual aspect in the psyche so deeply in himself and others, Jung could indeed truthfully say that the question had been with him since the beginning.

In *Answer to Job*, Jung is speaking not metaphysically but psychologically. He's showing us something about the nature of our images of the divine and of our ourselves. The book looks at an ongoing pattern in the Bible in which the human characters lead the story's moral action. Jung focuses on Job, but believes that the story begins with Abraham and necessitates a fuller symbolic expression in Jesus.

In considering such material, Jung knows he's going to offend readers, but it's surprising to see how many different ways it could offend people. Rationalists found themselves offended by how seriously he took the God-image: 'Grow up! You expect too much. The world isn't like that!' thought the Jungian analyst and author Edward Edinger at first.[122] Knowing this, Jung opens the book with elaborate courtesy, begging the indulgence of the kind reader.

He asks people to keep in mind the difference between physical truths and psychological ones. But he also opens that section with a quotation from the biblical story of King David: 'I am distressed for thee my brother.' This points to the fact that Jung knows he's walking into a profound conflict within our culture – one that is

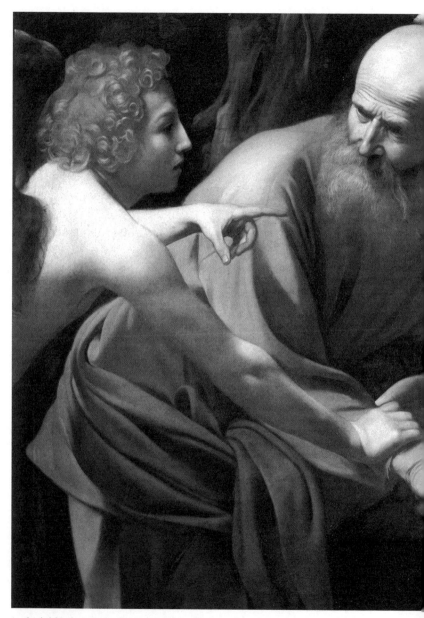

In the biblical story, God instructed Abraham to sacrifice his son, Isaac. In Jung's view, this was not just a test of faith for Abraham, but also a means of God expressing his own conflicted nature.

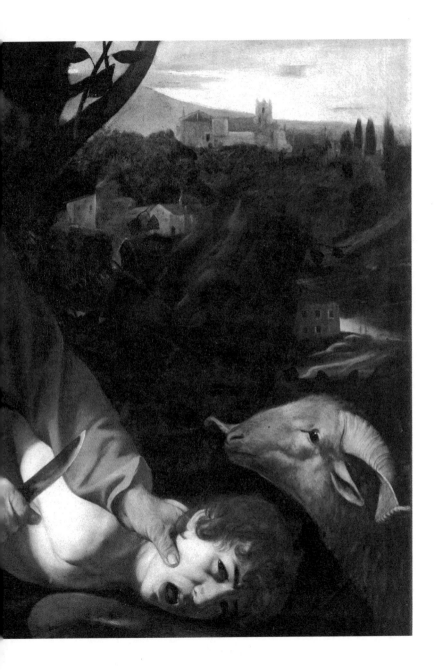

alive and well in many of us. Even if he asks nicely, he knows he's about to push some very deep buttons inside of us.

The biblical Book of Job opens with God bragging to Satan about how faithful Job is. Satan's response is basically 'Sure he's faithful now, when you've blessed him with everything, but let's see what happens when you take all that away from him.' 'You're on,' says God, and the story of the pitiful Job begins.

In short order, circumstances conspire to relieve Job of his herds, his servants, his sons and daughters. Yet he remains faithful. In a negotiation reminiscent of *The Godfather*, Satan returns to God to check in before inflicting more, and receives the limit: 'but save his life'. Going forth, he serves up a head-to-toe case of boils, and Job must scrape these with a shard of glass while sitting in the ashes of his former home.

Job's wife tells him he should 'curse God and die'. Three friends arrive to grieve with him, and they sit with him for a week before anyone speaks. Needless to say, Job is bitter, but he still doesn't curse God. His friends discuss the situation with him but provide little help, 'miserable comforters are ye all'. The problem is that they see, in the words of a *New York Times* review, that Job 'expected God to help him against God'. Job prepares himself to face God: 'I will speak in the bitterness of my soul. I will say unto God, "Do not condemn me; show me wherefore thou contendest with me. Is it good unto thee that thou shouldest oppress, that thou shouldest despise the work of thine hands, and shine upon the counsel of the wicked? Hast thou eyes of flesh? or seest thou as man seeth?"'

Although Job is now defeated and crushed, God answers him not with any explanation but instead by appearing in a whirlwind and proclaiming his mightiness, his great power, his 'terrible majesty'. He shows him the powerful animal nature of Leviathan. Perhaps worst of all, he 'goes unconscious', pretending that it is Job who is lacking in understanding.

But Job sees clearly. He knows precisely what has happened to him and whose fault it is. God reveals himself to Job in all his frightfulness. 'Job realizes God's inner antinomy . . . by his insistence on bringing his case before God, even without hope of a hearing, had stood his ground and thus created the very obstacle that forced God to reveal his true nature.'[123]

Could God have a shadow? Does God include within him the Devil? Does humanity suffer God so that His shadow might become known to him? Such an understanding brings living purpose to our struggle against evil, and dignifies moral action and our struggle for consciousness.

Jung saw early evidence for this in Genesis when Abraham petitions God not to destroy Sodom and Gomorrah in case there are good people who will be killed along with the bad. Here, Abraham leads God towards greater mercy. Later in Genesis, God instructs Abraham to bind his first son Isaac in preparation for sacrifice to him. At the last moment, a ram appears and a messenger from God tells him to sacrifice the ram instead. Again, God's own conflicted nature is being tested through Abraham's faith.

Jung turned to the Jewish Midrashic literature to look for evidence of self-critical reflection in the Deity, and found one late example there. 'Yahweh [God] asks for the blessing of the high priest Ishmael, and Ishmael answer him: "May it be Thy will that Thy mercy may suppress Thy anger, and that Thy compassion may prevail over Thy other attributes . . ." The Almighty feels that a truly sanctified man is superior to himself.'[124]

This conflict reveals itself most explicitly in Job. 'Yahweh did wrong but didn't recognize it . . . Job is certainly conscious of divine injustice and thus is more conscious than Yahweh. It is the subtle superiority of man's advance in moral consciousness *vis-à-vis* a less conscious God.'[125] Jung recognized that Job's suffering does not merely bring him to a clearer understanding of God; that new understanding must also affect God. 'It just could not be that Yahweh's dual nature should become public property and remain hidden from himself alone. Whoever knows God has an effect on him.'[126] This process anticipates the God-become-man belief of Christianity, and the idea that humanity plays a role in the divine drama is also found in Gnosticism and elsewhere.[127]

The Athi Plains in Nairobi National Park, Kenya, which Jung visited in 1925, is home to a large population of antelope and zebra.

Rivkah Kluger, an analysand and student of Jung's with a doctoral degree in Semitic Languages and the History of Religion, wrote that Jung described it to her this way: 'Through the suffering that he inflicted upon Job out of his own nature, God has come to his self-knowledge . . . And that is what redeems the man Job. This is really the solution to the enigma of Job, that is, a true justification for Job's fate, which, without this background, would in its cruelty and injustice remain an open problem. Job appears here clearly as a sacrifice, but also as the carrier of the divine fate, and that gives meaning to his suffering and liberation to his soul.'[128]

That is the 'service which man can render to God, that light may emerge from the darkness, that the Creator may become conscious of himself. That is the one goal which fits man meaningfully into the scheme of creation, and at the same time covers meaning upon it.'[129]

Jung saw that humanity had a role to play in reflecting creation back to the Creator. This was not just a philosophical concept for Jung, but an embodied emotional vision that struck him powerfully during his 1925 visit to Africa. There, he stood upon the Athi Plains facing gigantic herds of gazelle, antelope and zebra. Leaving his companions behind, he stared upon the world much as it had been since the very beginning:

There the cosmic meaning of consciousness became overwhelmingly clear to me . . . Man, I, in an invisible act of creation put the stamp of perfection on the world by giving it objective existence. This act we usually ascribe to the Creator alone . . . Now I knew what it was, and knew even more: that man is indispensable for the completion of creation; that, in fact, he himself is the second creator of the world, who alone has given to the world its objective existence without which, unheard, unseen, silently eating, giving birth, dying, heads nodding through hundreds of millions of years, it would have gone on in the profoundest night of non-being down to its unknown end. Human consciousness created objective existence and meaning, and man found his indispensable place in the great process of being.[130]

Jung sees a profound place for humanity in the ongoing divine drama. He sees God as needing humanity, and humanity as needing God. In a more adult-to-adult view of the sacred, each side needs the other to advance. While placing humanity into the divine drama is a challenging notion for some, it gives purpose to our drive for consciousness and for moral action. Every step we take with awareness is one that brings the cosmic shadow to light and becomes a grain of sand on a universal scale. As Edward Edinger noted, 'The new myth postulates that the created universe and its most exquisite flower, humanity, make up a vast enterprise for the creation of consciousness, that each individual is a unique experiment in that process; and that sum total of consciousness created by each individual is deposited as a permanent addition to the collective treasury.'[131]

When astronauts landed on the Moon in 1969, they demonstrated the extraordinary power held by humanity. In these times, Jung's call for us to face our collective shadow is more important than ever.

While each of us can decide spiritual questions for ourselves, the psychological questions of our age point towards the necessity of considering Jung's new understanding. In our time, we hold the power of the Gods like no previous human generation. Since the atomic age, we have held the power of life and death over the planet. Metaphorically, in our flight to the Moon we touched the face of the Gods for the first time in our history. In coming to see what we've done to the planet with climate change, we are being forced to face our civilizational shadow, the fact that our dominant institutions are not life-generating, but life-destroying. 'Modern man must discover a deeper source of his own spiritual life. To do this he is obliged to struggle with evil, to confront his shadow, to integrate the Devil. There is no other choice.'[132] We must face the evil in ourselves and in our culture. We must admit that we do hold power over life and death for the planet and ourselves. Without acknowledging that we hold the power of the Gods in a way like never before, we may express the shadow side of those forces unconsciously with terrible consequences. 'The world hangs by a thin thread, and that thread is the psyche of man . . . We are the great danger.'

For those interested engaging with *Answer to Job* and Edinger's in-depth interpretations, *The Creation of Consciousness and The Transformation of the God-Image* are required reading.

THE LAST YEARS

In September 1939, Freud passed away in London. Jung would continue to praise him and acknowledge his contribution to Western thought for the rest of his life. Toni Wolff died in March 1953, and her death stunned Jung. To honour her, he carved a stone memorial with the Chinese characters 'Lotus Nun Mysterious'. Emma Jung died two years later in 1955, and Jung carved a stone memorial for her too. Of course, the loss of these two women changed the character of Jung's life for his final years. From this point on, his children would come to stay with him at the house in Küsnacht to keep him company.

Carl Gustav Jung died on 6 June 1961 at his home. At the time of his death, a thunderstorm covered Lake Zurich and lightning split a magnificent poplar tree under which he had often sat to read. This synchronicity was echoed years later, when his good friend Laurens van der Post was being interviewed for a documentary film on Jung: 'When the moment came for me to speak directly to the camera about Jung's death, and I came to the description of how the lightning demolished Jung's favourite tree, the lightning struck again in the garden. The thunder crashed out so loudly that I winced, and to this day the thunder, wince, and the impediment of speech it caused are there in the film for all to see, just as the lightning is visible on the screen over the storm-tossed lake and wind-whipped trees.'[133]

Soon after Jung died, a poplar tree in his garden was struck by lightning.

SYNCHRONICITY

◎ Key Points

- **Alchemy** – Jung saw a relationship between the processes and stages of alchemy and our psychological development. His 1944 book *Psychology and Alchemy* explores alchemy as a metaphor for individuation. *Mysterium Coniunctionis* (1963) focuses on the sacred marriage between the archetypal Masculine and Feminine.

- **Synchronicity** – a term coined by Jung to refer to the meaningful interrelation of outer events with inner psychological states. These events often happen during emotionally charged times, and often direct us towards something that needs to brought into awareness. Recognizing that places and objects can be brought into purposive arrangement to reflect the development of consciousness forces us to look at the nature of reality in a new way.

- *Answer to Job* – this 1952 book by Jung considers the moral and psychological implications of the Book of Job. Jung observes that throughout the Bible it is the human characters that lead the ethical development. Job's story, like Abraham's and Jesus's, leads God [Yahweh] to face his own dark side. This understanding places humanity meaningfully into the divine drama, and gives a purposive explanation for evil and our drive for moral action and consciousness.

Appendix I

Carl Jung and World War II

It is now known that during World War II Jung aided the Allies by delivering psychological profiles of the Axis leaders to Mary Bancroft, who passed them along to Allen Dulles of the Office of Strategic Services (OSS) — the predecessor to the CIA. Dulles recognized the tremendous importance of Jung's contributions.

There have been accusations made against Jung of anti-Semitism, both during and following the war. These stem from his editorship of *Zentralblatt*, the journal of the General Medical Society for Psychotherapy. When the Nazis came to power in 1933, Jung took over the editorship of the journal in the hopes of preventing it from falling under their control. He made the society an international rather than German organization and broke the society up into national groups, to reduce their influence. These steps were not publicly known.

In December 1933, a German edition of the journal included a pro-Nazi supplement without Jung's approval or awareness. Throughout the 1930s, Jung and his later co-editor C.A. Meier included articles and reviews of work by Jewish authors. His 1937 work *Psychology and Religion* warned of the dangers of the mass movement in Germany. He wrote a foreword to a book by his French Jewish student Jolande Jacobi, which came out in 1939. In 1940, Jung resigned his post and the organization fell entirely under Nazi control. After this time, Jung was blacklisted in Germany and his writings were suppressed. Jung feared a

German invasion of Switzerland throughout the war. Having been blacklisted, he knew that his capture would have likely led to his death. 'On account of my critical utterances I was "marked down" by the Gestapo, my books were banned in Germany, and in France they were for the most part destroyed.'[134]

Aniela Jaffé, Jung's secretary, explores these allegations more fully in her book *From the Life and Work of C.G. Jung*. Herself a Jew, she had begun analysis with Jung in 1938. He helped her to escape Germany and gave her employment – at first with the Psychological Club and later with him. Allegations of anti-Semitism against Jung also overlook that he chose as his mentor Sigmund Freud, who was both Jewish and rejected by the medical establishment of the time, and that throughout his life some of his closest professional and personal collaborators were Jewish.

Accusations of racism against Jung are unfortunate, not only because they keep people who might otherwise be interested from reading his books, but because Jung was someone who celebrated world cultures and world mythology. He promoted non-European scholarly works, writing forewords to the *The Secret of the Golden Flower* (a classic Taoist text) and the *I Ching*. He advocated for the rights of Native Americans, calling for them to be granted full citizenship in 1932. He also recognized the savagery of what had been done to them, saying that 'if a Pueblo Indian should one day say to me "You Europeans are worse than ravaging beasts," I would have to agree politely.'[135] Jung accepted complicity in the atrocities done to them. He hated the idea of missionaries being sent to pull indigenous people from their roots and chafed so much at people speaking badly about Africans that he left a party because of it. This was witnessed by Laurens van der Post, who wrote that Jung loved Africa because 'it had finally settled whatever doubts he might have had of the validity and universality of an area of the human spirit shared by all men, no matter how different their cultures, their creeds, and their races and colours, an area for which he had coined the term *collective unconscious*.[13]

Appendix II
A Field Guide to Jung Today

As mentioned in the Introduction, the Jungian community is a worldwide, organically growing phenomenon. The tradition of Jungian psychology is kept alive not only by analysts, psychotherapists and their patients, but also by a broad network of organizations, academics, artists, writers, business people, theologians, scientists and others. It includes millions of readers of the works, not only of Jung, but of the many influential authors who carry the approach forward in their own ways. The expanse of this great family is far too vast to describe, but there are a few ongoing organizations that are at the centre of Jungian life today (and an advance apology to any group we have missed).

The backbone of this ecosystem are the Institutes. Jungian Institutes worldwide provide clinical training that integrates modern psychotherapeutic approaches with the depth of traditional Jungian insight. In addition to psychological course work, training analysts are required to have completed 50–100 hours of personal analysis before beginning the programme, and another 300 during it. Because they complete both an extensive personal analysis – where they work on themselves – and an excellent psychological education, programme graduates know 'the pipes', they have a lived familiarity with the dynamics of the unconscious. That understanding makes them helpful guides for those venturing on their own similar journeys.

The International Association for Analytical Psychology is the organizing body of Jungian analysts, and it is based in Zurich. The IAAP hosts an annual congress every year and has associations or affiliates in 58 countries (iaap.org). The IAAP website lists group members across the world, including South Africa, Japan, Korea, Australia, Venezuela, Mexico, Brazil, Argentina and all across Europe, Canada and the United States.

The original Jungian Institute in Zurich remains a primary hub of the movement, offering courses for both clinicians and the general public (www.junginstitut.ch). Also found there is the International School of Analytical Psychology Zurich (www.isapzurich.com), as well as the Jung von Franz centre (www.jungvonfranz.center).

There are Jung Institutes offering analytic training and offering excellent public programmes in New York, Boston, Los Angeles, San Francisco, Chicago, Dallas and Pittsburgh, as well as the Interregional Society of Jungian Analysts in the United States, London, Berlin and across Europe, and ones in Canada, Israel, France, Mexico and Brazil. There are developing groups of interested clinicians and others in Asia, Latin America and Central and Eastern Europe. There are also a variety of split-off associations and groups within the larger Jungian family, including several different organizations in London, New York and Los Angeles.

The Jung family actively curates the legacy of C.G. Jung's published works. They are assisted in developing new material to be published from the archives by the Philemon Foundation, a US non-profit organization (philemonfoundation.org). The family has also opened up the family home in Küsnacht for reserved ticket tours (www.cgjunghaus.ch).

Pacifica Graduate Institute is a major West Coast North American hub of the Jungian world. It offers graduate programmes in Jungian-oriented psychology and related disciplines on two campuses near Santa Barbara, CA. It offers widely attended public programmes and conferences, and is the home of the archives of

Joseph Campbell, James Hillman, Marija Gimbutas and Marion Woodman (www.pacifica.edu). Pacifica's founding president, Dr Stephen Aizenstat (dreamtending.com), also began the Global Dream Initiative, which brings together a network of dreamers to listen to the psyche for healing possibilities for the world (www.globaldreaminitiative.com).

Other Jungian-oriented graduate schools and course offerings include: in the UK, the University of Essex offers an MA in Jungian and Post-Jungian studies; in Toronto, Canada, the New College offers Interdisciplinary Courses in Jungian Theory; in California, Saybrook, CIIS (www.ciis.edu) and Sonoma State offer programmes.

Scholarly organizations include: Jungian Society for Scholarly Studies (www.jungiansociety.org); and the *International Journal of Jungian Studies* (IJJS), which bridges the professional, clinical, and academic worlds of Jungian Studies for an international audience, among others.

A network of wonderful local organizations are the grassroots of the Jungian organism. The Houston Jung Center (junghouston.org) is long-time leader in excellent programmes, but societies and groups span the globe, from the San Diego Friends of Jung (jungsandiego.org) to the Jung Centre in Dublin (www.jungcentre.com) and from the Southern Alabama Friends of Jung (friendsofjungsouth.org) to the Comox Valley C.G. Jung Society (comoxjung.com) in British Columbia, Canada. Check for one close to you!

There are also many new and/or web-based organizations within the Jungian world. Depth Psychology Alliance is a large community offering discussion, online events and courses (www.depthpsychologyalliance.com). In Europe, Stillpoint Spaces hosts live events for the public and online events, and offers a therapist referral service with clinicians of all-depth psychological stripes (www.stillpointspaces.com). Jungian Online refers clients who want to work with Jungian analysts and therapists via live video, and hosts online talks and other events (www.jungianonline.

com). In South Africa and online, The Centre for Applied Jungian Studies offers accessible courses (appliedjung.com). Jung Archademy is an online school offering hybrid video/live courses for personal growth, whose faculty includes psychologists, academics and Jungian analysts (www.jungarchademy. com). And finally, the very popular and insightful *This Jungian Life* podcast features three analysts in dialogue each episode (www.thisjungianlife.com).

Chronology of Jung's Life and Publications

1875	Carl Gustav Jung is born in Kesswil, Switzerland on 26 July.
1879	The Jung family moved to Kleinhüngingen near Basel.
1895 –1900	Jung studies medicine at the University of Basel.
1896	His father dies on 28 January.
1900	Began working as second assistant to well-known psychiatrist Eugen Bleuler at Burghölzli Clinic psychiatric hospital in Zurich.
1902	Becomes second assistant at the Burghölzli. Doctoral thesis in medicine, *On the Psychology and Pathology of So-called Occult Phenomenon.*
1902–3	Winter semester studies with Pierre Janet at the Salpétrière.
1903	Marries Emma Rauschenbach (born 1882); Together they would have five children.
1905–9	Clinical director at the Burghölzli.
1905–13	Professor at the Faculty of Medicine of Zurich, teaches psychiatry.
1907	*The Psychology of Dementia Praecox* (on schizophrenia). Meets Sigmund Freud in Vienna in February.
1909–13	Editor-in-chief of primary journal of psychoanalysis.
1909	Opens private practice in Küsnacht. Travels to Clark University in Massachusetts with Freud to lecture.
1910–13	Confrontation with unconscious period.
1910	Meets Antonia "Toni" Wolff.
1912	Lectures at Fordham University in New York City. *Symbols of Transformation.* Breaks with Freud.
1913	Resigns from teaching post at University of Zurich.
1917	Begins mandala drawing practice.
1918–19	Commander of prisoner of war camp for English soldiers.

1921 *Psychological Types.*

1923 Begins building tower at Bollingen on Lake Zurich.
Death of his mother.
Richard Wilhelm presents on the I Ching at Zurich Psychological Club.

1924–5 Travels to the United States, visits the Pueblo Indians of New Mexico.

1925–6 Expedition to Africa. Visits the Elgonyis at Mount Elgon.

1928 *The Relations between the Ego and Unconscious.*
On Psychic Energy.

1929 Commentary on *The Secret of the Golden Flower.*

1935 Professor at the Polytechnical School at the University of Zurich.
Founds the Swiss Society for Applied Psychology.
Tavistock lectures in London.

1936 Awarded honorary doctorate from Harvard.

1937 Terry Lectures at Yale.

1938 Voyage to India.

1940 *Psychology and Religion.*

1941 *Essays on the Science of Mythology* with C. Kerenyi.

1942 Resigns from professorship at the Polytechnical School.

1944 *Psychology and Alchemy.*

1946 *Psychology of the Transference.*

1948 Founding of the C. G. Jung Institute in Zürich.

1951 *Aion.*

1952 *Synchronicity: An Acausal Connecting Principle.*
Answer to Job.

1953 Death of Antonia "Toni" Wolff on March 21.
First volume of *The Collected Works* in English.

1955 Death of his wife Emma on November 27.

1956 Mysterium Coniunctionis.

1957 *The Undiscovered Self.*

1961 Finishes "Approaching the Unconscious" in *Man and His Symbols.*
Dies ten days later on June 6th at his home in Küsnacht.

Notes

Introduction

1   Carl Jung, *Collected Works*, vol. 13 (Princeton University Press, 1970–79), par. 119

2   Deirdre Bair, *Jung: A Biography* (Little Brown, 2003), p. 493

3   Carl Jung, *The Undiscovered Self* (Princeton University Press, 1957) p. 78

Chapter 1: Jung's Psychology

4   C. Hall and V. Nordby, *A Primer of Jungian Psychology* (Taplinger Publishing Company, 1973), p. 29

5   Aniela Jaffé, *From the Life and Work of C.G. Jung* (Daimon Verlag, 1989), p. 113

6   Hall and Nordby, *A Primer of Jungian Psychology*, p. 64

7   E.A. Bennet, *What Jung Really Said* (Schocken Books, 1966), p. 34

8   June Singer, *Boundaries of the Soul* (Penguin Books, 1972), p. 44

9   Jung, *Collected Works*, vol. 3, par. 84

10   Ibid., vol. 8, par. 96

11   Bennett, *What Jung Really Said*, p. 42

12   Jung, *Collected Works*, vol. 8, p. 225

13   Ibid., vol. 7, p. 287

14   Ibid., *Collected Works*, vol. 15, par. 119

15   Carl Jung, *Memories, Dreams, Reflections* (Penguin Books, 1961), p. 140

16   Carl Jung, quoted by Singer in *Boundaries of the Soul*, p. 8

17   Robert A. Johnson, *Inner Work* (Harper Collins, 1981), p. 4

Chapter 2: The Shadow

18   Singer, *Boundaries of the Soul*, p. 36

19   Ibid., p. 164

20   Ibid., p. 159

21   Jung, *Collected Works*, vol. 9, part i, par. 221

22   Singer, *Boundaries of the Soul*, pp. 164–5

23   Elie Humbert, *C.G. Jung: The Fundamentals of Theory and Practice* (Chiron Publications, 1988), p. 49

24   Jung, *Memories, Dreams, Reflections*, p. 246

25   Connie Zweig and Jeremiah Abrams, *Meeting the Shadow: The Hidden Power of the Dark Side of Human Nature* (Penguin, 1991)

26   Jung, *The Undiscovered Self*, p. 110

27   Robert A. Johnson, *Owning Your Own Shadow* (Harper, 1994), p. 4

28   Humbert, *C.G. Jung*, p. 48

29   Carl Jung, *Collected Works*, vol. 9, part ii, par. 423

30   Ibid., vol. 11, par. 134

31   Ann Belford Ulanov, *The Wisdom of the Psyche* (Paulist Press, 1971), pp. 35–6

Chapter 3: Inner Work

32   Jung, *Collected Works*, vol. 10, par. 318

33   Robert Bosnak, *A Little Course in Dreams* (Shambhala Publications, 1988), p. 7

34   Jung, *Collected Works*, vol. 18, par. 52
35   Deb Powers, https://dreamtending.com/blog/most-important-terms-mean-ing-of-dreams/
36   Carl Jung, *Letters*, vol. 1, pp. 28–9
37   Andrew Samuels, Bani Shorter and Fred Plaut, *A Critical Dictionary of Jungian Analysis* (Routledge & Kegan Paul, 1986), p. 9
38   Humbert, *C.G. Jung*, pp. 25–6
39   Singer, *Boundaries of the Soul*, p. 288
40   Ann Belford Ulanov, speaking at Spirituality and Religion Conference, San Francisco Jung Society, 2003
41   Singer, *Boundaries of the Soul*, p. 312
42   Jung, *Collected Works*, vol. 9, part ii, par. 14
43   Ibid., vol. 11, par. 292
44   Singer, *Boundaries of the Soul*, p. 312
45   Becca Tarnas, 'The Back of Beyond: The Red Books of C.G. Jung and J.R.R. Tolkien', (Ph.D. diss., California Institute of Integral Studies, 2018)
46   Elisabeth Pomès, IAAP, private communication
47   Humbert, *C.G. Jung*, pp. 29–30
48   Johnson, *Inner Work*, p. 100

Chapter 4: The Self
49   Jung, *Collected Works*, vol. 11, par. 390
50   C.G. Jung and William McGuire, *C.G. Jung Speaking: Interviews and Encounters* (Princeton University Press, 1987), p. 328
51   Singer, *Boundaries of the Soul*, p. 240
52   Ibid., p. 218
53   Ulrich Hoerni, Thomas Fischer, and Bettina Kaufmann (eds.), *The Art of C.G. Jung* (W.W. Norton, 2018), p. 120
54   Carl Jung, *Flying Saucers: A Modern Myth of Things Seen in the Skies* (Princeton University Press, 1959)
55   Gary Bobroff, *Crop Circles, Jung & the Reemergence of the Archetypal Feminine* (North Atlantic, 2014)
56   Lionel Corbett, *The Religious Function of the Psyche* (Chiron Books, 1996), pp. 46–7
57   Jung and McGuire, *C.G. Jung Speaking*, p. 401
58   Barbara Hannah, *Jung: His Life and Work*, p. 115
59   Jung, *Memories, Dreams, Reflections*, p. 209
60   Humbert, *C.G. Jung*, p. 122
61   Laurens van der Post, *Jung and The Story of Our Time* (Penguin, 1975), p. 177
62   Jung, *Collected Works*, vol. 16, par. 452
63   Ibid., vol 14, par. 756
64   Ibid., vol. 7, par. 509
65   Mare-Louise von Franz, *Archetypal Dimensions of the Psyche* (Penguin, 1997), p. 98
66   Jung, *Collected Works*, vol. 8, par. 514
67   Ibid., vol. 8, par. 459
68   Ibid., vol. 18, par. 1099

Chapter 5: Personality Types
69   Jung, *Collected Works*, vol. 6, p. v
70   Humbert, *C.G. Jung*, p. 109
71   Jung, *Collected Works*, vol. 6, pars. 976f

72   Carl Jung, *Dream Analysis 1: Notes of the Seminar Given in 1928–30* (Routledge, Taylor & Francis Books, 1984), p. 75
73   Jung and McGuire, *C.G. Jung Speaking*, p. 309
74   Jung, *Collected Works*, vol. 17, par. 359

Chapter 6: Archetypes
75   Jung, *Memories, Dreams, Reflections*, p. 182
76   Jung, *Collected Works*, vol. 8, p. 112
77   Carl Jung, *Man and His Symbols* (Routledge, 1984), p. 57
78   Marie-Louise von Franz, *Projection and Re-collection in Jungian Psychology* (Open Court, 1980), p. 85
79   Jung, *Collected Works*, vol. 9, part i, par. 404
80   Carl Jung, 'Protocols' for Memories, Dreams, Reflections (1958)
81   Jung, *Collected Works*, vol. 9, part i, par. 289
82   Carl Jung, *Answer to Job* (Princeton University Press, 1952), par. 742

Chapter 7: Anima and Animus
83   Carl Jung, 'Marriage as a Psychological Relationship', (1925) in *Collected Works*, vol. 17, par. 338
84   Carl Jung, *The Red Book* (W.W. Norton, 2009), p. 263
85   Jung, *Collected Works*, vol. 13, p. 60
86   Ulanov, *The Wisdom of the Psyche*, pp. 42–3
87   Marie-Louise von Franz, *The Interpretation of Fairy Tales* (Shambhala, 1970)
88   Daniel J. Meckel and Robert L. Moore, *Self and Liberation: The Jung-Buddhism Dialogue* (Paulist Press, 1992), p. 313
89   Erich Neumann, *The Origins and History of Consciousness* (Princeton University Press, 1959), p. 121
90   Jeffrey Raff, *Jung and the Alchemical Imagination* (Nicolas-Hays, 2000), p. 102
91   Jung, *Collected Works*, vol. 5, par. 344
92   Anne Baring and Jules Cashford, *The Myth of the Goddess: Evolution of an Image* (Viking, 1991), p. 66
93   Ulanov, *The Wisdom of the Psyche*, p. 133
94   Jung, *Collected Works*, vol. 10, par. 295
95   E. Gadon, *The Once and Future Goddess* (Harper One, 1989), p. 76
96   Baring and Cashford, *The Myth of the Goddess*, p. 66
97   Esther M. Harding, *Women's Mysteries Ancient and Modern* (Putnam, 1935), p. 42
98   Marja Reinau, *Love Matters for Psychic Transformation* (Fisher King Press, 2016), foreword
99   Richard Tarnas, *The Passion of the Western Mind* (Penguin Random House, 1991), epilogue
100   Carl Jung, *Civilization in Transition* (Princeton University Press, 1970), par. 585
101   Carl Jung, *The Spiritual Problem of Modern Man* (Princeton University Press), par. 154
102   Robert Johnson, *We: Understanding the Psychology of Romantic Love* (Harper Collins, 1983), p. 76
103   Tarnas, *The Passion of the Western Mind*, epilogue
104   'The Geography of the Soul. An Interview with Marie-Louise von Franz', *Jungian Directions, Newsletter of the C.G. Jung Society of Vancouver*, Winter–Spring 1994, pp. 2–5

Chapter 8: Synchronicity

105   Monika Wikman, *Pregnant Darkness: Alchemy and the Rebirth of Consciousness* (Nicolas-Hays, 2004), p. xxii
106   Jung and McGuire, *C.G. Jung Speaking*, p. 229
107   Samuels, Shorter and Plaut, *A Critical Dictionary of Jungian Analysis*, p. 12
108   Cynthia Cavalli, 'An Exploration of objective meaning in transformational synchronicities', *International Journal of Human Resources Development and Management* (2013)
109   Polly Young-Eisendrath and Terence Dawson, *The Cambridge Companion to Jung* (Cambridge University Press, 1997), p. 311
110   Jung, *Memories, Dreams, Reflections*, p. 155
111   Michael Shermer, 'Anomalous Events that Can Shake One's Skepticism to the Core', *Scientific American*, 1 October 2014
112   Ibid.
113   Jung, *Letters*, vol. ii, pp. 538–9
114   Richard Tarnas, *Cosmos and Psyche*, p. 56
115   Jaffé, *From the Life and Work of C.G. Jung* (Harper & Row, 1968), p. 45
116   Shermer, 'Anomalous Events that Can Shake One's Skepticism to the Core', *Scientific American*, 1 October 2014
117   J. Gary Sparks, *At the Heart of the Matter* (Inner City Books, 2007), p. 105
118   Marie-Louise von Franz, *Psyche and Matter* (Shambhala, 2001), p. 257
119   Tarnas, *Cosmos and Psyche*, p. 56
120   Ferne Jensen & Sidney Mullen (eds.), *C.G. Jung, Emma Jung and Toni Wolff – A Collection of Remembrances* (Analytical Psychology Club of San Francisco, 1982), p. 20
121   Sparks, *At the Heart of the Matter*, p. 55
122   Edward Edinger, *Transformation of the God-Image* (Inner City Books, 1992), p. 28
123   Jung, *Collected Works*, vol. 11, par. 584
124   Jung and McGuire, *C.G. Jung Speaking*, p. 226
125   Ibid., p. 227
126   Jung, *Answer to Job*, par. 617
127   Edward Edinger, *The Creation of Consciousness* (Inner City Books, 1984), p. 19
128   Rivkah Kluger, *Satan in the Old Testament* (Northwestern Univeristy Press, 1967), p. 129
129   Jung, *Memories, Dreams, Reflections*, p. 338
130   Ibid., pp. 253–74
131   Edinger, *The Creation of Consciousness*, p. 23
132   Jung and McGuire, *C.G. Jung Speaking*, p. 230
133   van der Post, *Jung and the Story of Our Time*, p. 275

Appendix I: Carl Jung and World War II

134   Jung, *Letters*, vol. 1, p. 404
135   Ibid., vol. 1, p. 370
136   van der Post, *Jung and the Story of Our Time*, pp. 48–9

Index

Picture Credits

Alamy: 21, 22

Bridgeman Images: 106

Diomedia: 85, 114

Getty Images: 41, 62, 96, 112, 150, 169

Library of Congress: 10, 76, 81, 110, 116

Public Domain: 8, 9, 14, 17, 25, 27, 28, 29, 31, 34, 46, 47, 52, 57, 59, 60, 66, 89, 108, 118, 126, 133, 142, 144, 151, 153, 155, 161, 173, 174, 178, 179, 183, 186, 189, 191, 197, 200, 208, 212, 214, 220

Shutterstock: 51, 55, 73, 78, 92, 102, 104, 119, 147, 176, 204, 211, 218, 222

Wellcome Collection: 35, 131, 135, 157, 159, 198, 206